Love at Its Best When Church Is a Mess

"*Love at its Best When Church is a Mess* is a book that is needed for the messy times that the church finds itself in today. Through conceptual analysis, warm stories, scriptural references, and personal questions, Patrick Allen leads the reader through a discovery of oneself. First Corinthians 13 is used as a mirror to see more clearly and practice more faithfully the gracious gift of God's love."

—**Stephen Green**, W. N. King Chair of Theology, Southern Nazarene University

"I love the way my friend Patrick Allen so clearly describes how church is both beautiful and messy, just like life. In my fourth decade of pastoral ministry I've seen lots of healthy and unhealthy behaviors played out in the faith community. I believe this book is helpful for those new to church, lifers in church, and those in between. Love, God's and ours, must remain central and Patrick shows us how to do it well."

—**Paul Almquist**, Senior Pastor, West Chehalem Friends Church, Newberg, Oregon

"With an engaging personal prose that perfectly balances seriousness and playfulness, Patrick Allen provides fresh insight on 1 Corinthians 13 and its charge for Christians today. This book is about the cultivation of virtue—the faith, hope, and love that define the journey from ourselves toward our home with God. Allen does not mince words or romanticize the journey; he is real and his authenticity is refreshing. Readers will treasure the wisdom in this book and discover the beauty that can emerge alongside our own restlessness and wandering."

—**Josh R. Sweeden**, Dean of the Faculty and Professor of Church and Society, Nazarene Theological Seminary

"Dr. Allen is amazing! This book has something for everyone seeking deeper discipleship. It's all there—wit, wisdom, and hope for the church in the twenty-first century. He brings Paul's message of love to life in such a powerful, hope-filled, practical way. This is good news for any age, but especially now as many grope for the essence of Christian community. I hope to apply this wisdom in my life and share it with my parish."

—**Tony Griffin**, Senior Pastor, First United Methodist Church, Russellville, Arkansas

"Ever witnessed a church divided, its members bickering, scheming, and taking up sides? What should be done? With keen insight, Patrick Allen unwraps the apostle Paul's gift to the church in times of crisis—1 Corinthians 13. Allen's work—refreshingly honest and exceedingly practical—invites the church, in the midst of its messy relational realities, into a more excellent way."

—**David Alexander**, former President, Northwest Nazarene University

Love at Its Best
When Church Is a Mess

Meditations from 1 Corinthians 13

Patrick Allen

CASCADE *Books* · Eugene, Oregon

LOVE AT ITS BEST WHEN CHURCH IS A MESS
Meditations from 1 Corinthians 13

Copyright © 2020 Patrick Allen. All rights reserved. Except for brief quotations in critical publications or reviews, no part of this book may be reproduced in any manner without prior written permission from the publisher. Write: Permissions, Wipf and Stock Publishers, 199 W. 8th Ave., Suite 3, Eugene, OR 97401.

Cascade Books
An Imprint of Wipf and Stock Publishers
199 W. 8th Ave., Suite 3
Eugene, OR 97401

www.wipfandstock.com

PAPERBACK ISBN: 978-1-7252-6774-9
HARDCOVER ISBN: 978-1-7252-6773-2
EBOOK ISBN: 978-1-7252-6775-6

Cataloguing-in-Publication data:

Names: Allen, Patrick, author.

Title: Love at its best when church is a mess : meditations from 1 Corinthians 13 / by Patrick Allen.

Description: Eugene, OR: Cascade Books, 2020

Identifiers: ISBN 978-1-7252-6774-9 (paperback) | ISBN 978-1-7252-6773-2 (hardcover) | ISBN 978-1-7252-6775-6 (ebook)

Subjects: LCSH: Bible. 1 Corinthians 13—Meditations. | Love—Religious aspects—Christianity.

Classification: BS2675 .A45 2020 (print) | BS2675 (ebook)

All Scripture quotations unless otherwise noted are taken from The Holy Bible, New International Version NIV. Copyright 1973, 1978, 1984, 2011 by Biblica, Inc. Used by Permission. All rights reserved worldwide.

Manufactured in the U.S.A.   09/29/20

This book is dedicated to my wife, Lori. When I think about unfailing love, her spirit and passion come immediately to mind. She is my partner, my biggest cheerleader, and my best friend.

For me, it all comes down to this:
Life is messy, but God is faithful.

Contents

Preface | ix
Introduction | xiii

Part I: The Heart And Soul Of Love | 1

Chapter 1: Love Is Patient | 3
Chapter 2: Love Is Kind | 18

Part II: Love Out Of Bounds | 31

Chapter 3: Love Does Not Envy | 33
Chapter 4: Love Does Not Boast | 43
Chapter 5: Love Is Not Proud | 53
Chapter 6: Love Does Not Dishonor Others | 64
Chapter 7: Love Is Not Self-Seeking | 75
Chapter 8: Love Is Not Easily Angered | 87
Chapter 9: Love Keeps No Record of Wrongs | 97
Chapter 10: Love Does Not Delight in Evil | 108

Part III: Love At Its Best | 117

Chapter 11: Love Rejoices With the Truth | 119
Chapter 12: Love Always Protects | 130
Chapter 13: Love Always Trusts | 137
Chapter 14: Love Always Hopes | 144
Chapter 15: Love Always Perseveres | 153

Conclusion: Love Never Fails | 161

Preface

WHEN YOU THINK OF the Apostle Paul, what words come to mind? For me, I think of this first great theologian and missionary of the church as a complex whirlwind—resolute and a bit stubborn, bold and yet tentative, passionate and a bit zealous, unrelenting and yet cautious, ordinary and a bit eccentric, wise and yet a simple traveling preacher. He was the first contributor to the New Testament, although I doubt that he ever intended to do so or had any idea that his letters would be a centerpiece not only for the fledging bands of believers he helped birth and loved so much, but also for Christian communities around the world for twenty-one centuries and counting. He was a curiosity to behold, especially given all that he experienced—anger, ridicule, rejection, betrayal, beatings, and imprisonment—and most of these more than once! As he slipped out of town and limped into the next city, who could have imagined that his preaching and teaching would literally change the world? All this, and he was a good tentmaker, too.

But I never thought of Paul as a poet, yet 1 Corinthians 13 is often described as a poem, a hymn, or an elegant inner movement of a symphony—a beautiful work of art. Honestly, when I first carefully read and pondered this passage, I concluded that it must have been written by someone else, perhaps Sosthenes, who is listed as a contributor or coauthor of this letter to the Corinthian church. It just didn't fit with my image of Paul. Yet, Pauline scholars generally agree that Paul is the author, a poet in disguise (my words, not theirs). Certainly, there is much more to this traveling preacher than first meets the eye.

There are misconceptions about the audience for 1 Corinthians 13, too. It is often called the Love Chapter, and rightly so. I can't even remember the last wedding I attended when some passage from this chapter was not shared in some way. Yet, Paul was not writing to engaged couples or to married couples celebrating a milestone anniversary, even though this chapter provides much inspiration and insight for lovers at all ages and stages of life. And neither was Paul writing about loving God or God's love for us.

Interestingly, in his writing, Paul urged Christians to love each other far more often than he called on them to love God.

This chapter, in fact, was written to Christians already a part of a community of faith in Corinth—those who claimed Christ, but things were not going very well. There was contention, confusion, jealousy, selfishness, pretense, and spiritual one-upmanship—not a happy place to worship. They were arguing about which prophet to follow, who should speak up and who should listen, what spiritual gifts were the most prestigious and how were they to be obtained and demonstrated, who were the most devout members, who should lead the congregation, and who should be silent when they gathered together, to mention just a few. It was to these believers and in this context that 1 Corinthians 13 was written. The love that Paul implores and prays for is a love that they were to have for each other—as Christians living in community, even if the community was a mess. And what makes this chapter so powerful is that it is equally applicable and indispensable for all of us who claim Christ today. Simply put, we are to love each other, and far too often we don't.

Love at Its Best When Church Is a Mess is a collection of fifteen meditations about various aspects of this love that Christians are called to extend to each other—and to exemplify. In Part I, we examine the heart and soul of love: patience (chapter 1) and kindness (chapter 2). These two virtues, according to the Apostle Paul, are indispensable. Without patience and kindness, love is hollow and incomplete, even phony. In Part II, we consider what happens when we make loving others more about us than about others, taking love out of bounds—envy (chapter 3), arrogance (chapter 4), pride (chapter 5), disrespect (chapter 6), self-centeredness (chapter 7), anger (chapter 8), counting wrongs (chapter 9), and delighting in evil (chapter 10). Part III offers aspects of love "at its best." First, we look at "rejoicing in the truth" (chapter 11) before turning to what love at its best always tries to do: protect (chapter 12), trust (chapter 13), hope (chapter 14), and persevere (chapter 15). No pretense will be offered that we can do these things perfectly. We can't. Thankfully, we are called to be faithful, not perfect.

At the end of the day, Paul tells us that three things remain: faith, hope, and love. We conclude this study together with some thoughts about their relationship: faith sends us on a spiritual journey, hope keeps us going, and love bids us home. Hopefully, this book will provide each of us with some stories to remember, some meditations to contemplate, some passages from Scripture to consider, and some spiritual disciplines and practices to incorporate as we make our way home, both literally and figuratively.

I want to end this preface with a disclaimer and a sincere hope. First, the disclaimer: I am not a biblical scholar, nor do I claim to be one. As such,

PREFACE

this book is not an analysis of the original language or an attempt to exegete Paul's intent from this text. This is a task for others to do, and honestly others have already done so at great length. Rather, this book is about appropriation—taking a line or idea and offering a story and a meditation about what it suggests to me. Hopefully, it will be memorable and helpful, too, as we all consider what it means to love each other as if our lives depended on it. In many ways, I think they do.

My sincere hope for this book is that readers will find occasion to both laugh and shed a tear or two as the result of the stories that I tell, mostly from my own personal experience. They are meant to offer a genuine human connection to the ideas that we will consider together. I simply tell the stories and leave it up to the readers to connect the dots. And I hope that the meditations and practical suggestions I offer will be helpful to all of us as we strive to make faith, hope, and love something honest and holy in our daily lives—and in our spiritual journeys, too. Actually, I believe that they are one and the same.

Patrick Allen
Newberg, Oregon
February 15, 2020

Introduction

If Is a Big Word

IF IS A POTENT word, a big word, and when used in conjunction with another word or phrase (which it usually is), its power is naturally amplified. For example, *if* paired with *only* can denote a sense of regret—*if only* I had listened to your advice, *if only* I knew the right thing to say, or *if only* I turned down that job offer from across the country that forced my family to relocate. We see this same regret demonstrated in the Gospel of John. Jesus did not immediately come when he received word that Lazarus was sick and was absent when Lazarus died. Both sisters, first Martha (11:21) and then Mary (11:32), said to Jesus when he finally arrived four days later, *if only* you had been here, my brother would not have died. In effect, where were you? Why didn't you come? We have followed you and you let us down. The sentiment and the sorrow of it all left Jesus in tears (11:35).

Even if can connote a sense of resignation or a severe limitation, as in *even if* I left home two hours earlier than usual, I still wouldn't have made the bus, or *even if* we had a million dollars, it wouldn't make the pain go away. But sometimes *even if* can be a statement of profound faith and commitment, too, as in the book of Daniel when three of Daniel's protégées, Shadrach, Meshach, and Abednego, were threatened with death by fire if they refused to bow down and worship King Nebuchadnezzar. They said to him, we believe that our God will deliver us, but *even if* he doesn't, we will not serve you (3:16–18). Or as my parents would tell me from time to time, *even if* you make a mess of things, you can always come home. We will be here for you—and I did, and they were.

And how many of us have looked to the future with anticipation: *if* I can get this job, *then* everything will be fine, *if* I graduate from college, *then* I will start working harder and showing up on time, or *if* the church hires some more staff, *then* I'll have time to take better care of myself. Of course, the trouble is that even when the *if* happens, the *then* is rarely as sweet or complete as we hoped it would be. Rather, far too often we have simply banked on the future at the expense of the present, and such investments rarely pay complete dividends.

Of course, *if-then* can also be a condition or a promise, as in the promise that the Lord made to King Solomon in 2 Chronicles 7:13–16: "When I shut up the heavens so that there is no rain, or command locusts to devour the land or send a plague among my people, *if* my people, who are called by my name, will humble themselves and pray and seek my face and turn from their wicked ways, *then* I will hear from heaven, and I will forgive their sin and will heal their land... My eyes and my heart will always be there." This last line is often omitted—it shouldn't be. What a wonderful promise.

On final pairing is worth noting—*if-but* . . ., signaling a certain incompleteness or insufficiency. Of course, the *if* portion may be all well and good; it is just not complete—it doesn't stand alone. It is in this sense that the Apostle Paul used this grammatical device in what are now the first three verses of 1 Corinthians 13: "*If* I speak in the tongues of men or of angels . . ." (1), "*If* I have the gift of prophecy . . ." (2); and "*If* I give all I possess to the poor . . ."(3); *but* do not have love . . . the "but" here is not coupled by accident.

Paul was attempting to answer some questions from a letter sent to him by the congregation in Corinth and trying as best he could to stave off problems he foresaw in the budding congregation. As he noted early in his response letter (1 Corinthians), "Jews demand signs and Greeks look for wisdom" (1:22). And since Corinth was under Roman control, we can add that the Romans obsession on gaining status and prominence, hoping to have a statue erected in your honor on the main street in town, was at play, too. So, in this one fledgling congregation, we see all types of conflict at work—some working to be seen as super spiritual, having a more direct connection with God; others promoting their own special knowledge, wisdom, insight, and debating skill; and still others wanting to be up front—to be seen as eloquent, powerful, and confident, visionary even, the qualities of a spiritual leader worthy of a statue in the marketplace. It was a perfect storm—a disaster waiting to happen. And happen it did.

The problem came to a head when the practice of various spiritual gifts emerged in Corinth. In effect, these new Christians were using their spiritual gifts as a way to promote their own special relationship with God, highlight their uncommon wisdom and insight, and demonstrate their extraordinary leadership capabilities—and, of course, to lord it over others in the congregation. It was a mess. Paul first affirmed the usefulness of various spiritual gifts for congregational life, and then carefully pointed out that the same God was at work in all of them. There would be no extra credit for any particular special gift (1 Cor 12), and then he pointed them all to "the most excellent way" (1 Cor 13:1).

This is where love finds its expression in Paul's thinking. Love is the most excellent way, available to everyone and expected from everyone. Love is to be pursued and practiced as the centerpiece of congregational life, not the pursuit of special spiritual gifts. To underscore the importance of love, Paul opens what is now 1 Corinthians 13 with a powerful series of *if-but* statements. His intent needs little explanation:

"*If* I speak in the tongues of men or of angels, **but** do not have love, I am only a resounding gong or a clanging cymbal. *If* I have the gift of prophecy and can fathom all mysteries and all knowledge, and *if* I have the faith that can move mountains, **but** do not have love I am nothing. *If* I give all I possess to the poor and give over my body to hardship that I may boast, **but** do not have love, I gain nothing." (13:1–3)

Simply put, you can produce all kinds of signs and wonders, bring wisdom and insight to the present and prophesy to the future, and speak with eloquence and passion in public, to name just a few, but without love at the core, these gifts are just a noisy distraction. They offer nothing helpful to the congregation, and there is nothing to be personally gained, either.

Indeed, this is a hard teaching. No wonder Paul writes 1 Corinthians 13 in such a lyrical style. For the Corinthians (and for most of us), the plain truth would be too stark, too harsh to take, so he packages the truth in a poem or perhaps in the words of a song, hoping that the beauty of it will allow the message to be received and accepted. It is a love song extended in love, a love that is to be desired and practiced—the very lifeblood of congregational life.

The Practice of Love

Assuming we accept Paul's message about the centrality of love to congregational life, it begs an obvious question: how do we practice this kind of love, so central to all of us who claim Christ as we worship and journey together? Here is where the hard work of 1 Corinthians 13 begins. Paul tells us straightaway about the two central practices that are the heart and soul of love—patience and kindness. That's where we begin, and it is hard work. Honestly, I often have a hard time being patient and kind with those I love, but Paul makes it clear that it is at the heart of congregational life as we know it. Wow! We will address these two practices in Part I.

And Paul doesn't just leave it there. He cautions us against bringing our own self-serving behaviors to the dance, making love more about ourselves than about others. Such things as envy, pride, anger, and keeping records of wrongs are simply out of bounds. In Part II: Love Out of Bounds, we'll consider eight different ways that our egos get in the way and think together about how we can stay within the boundaries of healthy relationships.

Third, we will examine what Love at Its Best looks like in Part III. We will note that the word *always* is a difficult standard, and most of us fail at one time or another. I will argue that "that's life" and we are called to be faithful, not perfect. This may cause some cognitive dissonance, but if you stay with me, I believe we'll be on the same page by the end of the book.

Finally, we'll conclude with a meditation on the combined power of *if-and*, the beauty and sway of spiritual gifts that are centered and anchored in love. And we will end with some reflections on Paul's statement that spiritual gifts are temporal. That is to say, at the end of the day they will cease, be stilled, pass away, be put away, or be recognized as limited, but three things remain—faith, hope, and love. And the greatest, according to Paul, is love (1 Cor 13:8–13).

I know that I lack the poetic power of the great apostle, but I would put it this way: Faith sends us on a spiritual journey; hope keeps us going; and love bids us home. May we all journey and rest in the promise that God's love will never fail us. Never. His eyes and his heart will always be with us. Deo gratias.

PART I

The Heart and Soul of Love

When I first joined the Boy Scouts, I had to memorize and promise to obey the Scout Law, but I really didn't know what I was getting myself into. A Scout is trustworthy, the list began, and after some consideration I thought that I could do that on a regular basis by keeping my promises, showing up on time, and keeping any confidences that my friends might share with me, not that many did. A Scout is loyal, helpful, friendly, and courteous, the list continued, and again, after reflecting on each attribute, I felt that I had a notion about what to do to practice them consistently. Then came kindness—a Scout is kind. This was troubling. The others on the list required me to *do* something, but this required me to *be* something, too. I was to be kind, and that would take some inner work on my part, but I didn't know how to summon that kind of quality.

I talked to my mother about my concerns, and she agreed that being kind was not the same type of outward activity like helping an old lady across the street or greeting my neighbors with a wave and a friendly smile. She said that kindness was deeper than that, associated with certain behaviors to be sure, but the behaviors had to be fueled and guided by something from within—an inner compass. Being kind, as she saw it, was an inside-out activity. It started with the heart, with the kind of person you are as an evidence of your spirit and goodness. I told her that this all seemed very demanding, and she agreed before adding, "You should just be thankful that patience is not on the list, too. That would be double trouble!"

Now I don't know if my mother, who read the Bible faithfully every day, was thinking of 1 Corinthians 13 at the time, but there is the pairing: Love is patient, love is kind . . . (4a). According to the Apostle Paul, patience and kindness are the cornerstones for love in the Christian community. Cornerstones are the most basic, essential part on which something's success, existence, or truth depends. If Paul is correct, and I think he is, love cannot exist without them. That makes patience and kindness serious business, holy business, for all of us, for the truth of our communal life depends on their expression within each of us and within our community of faith. For those who claim Christ, these two virtues are not optional. In essence, our love is defined by the kindness and patience we extend to each other, and to ourselves, too.

It isn't entirely clear to me why Paul chose patience and kindness to describe love, and it isn't clear why he emphasized faith, hope, and love over the cardinal virtues from the Greeks—prudence, justice, fortitude, and temperance—when addressing the turmoil in and around this young Christian congregation in Corinth. They would have been familiar with the teachings of Plato and others, to be sure, but for a congregation in a deep mess, a mess much of their own making, simply offering the cardinal virtues was not the answer, as helpful as they would have been to assist in living a good life. Healing required something deeper—something holy. What was needed, in Paul's view, was God's presence and grace. What the congregation needed to summon within them and among them with God's help were faith, hope, and love—and love was to be the centerpiece.

It is with this understanding that we turn to patience and kindness in Part I, to the heart and soul of love. According to Paul, patience and kindness are sacred, healing practices for a congregation where individuals are competing for prominence and status by displaying spiritual signs and wonders, by demonstrating wisdom through theological one-upmanship and debate, and by seeking and gaining positions of leadership and influence. In other words, they are for a congregation in a mess. His letter was intended for the church in Corinth 2,000 years ago, but I can't help thinking that there is much here that describes our congregational life today. Thus, we begin.

— 1 —

Love Is Patient

> The word patience means the willingness to stay where we are
> and live the situation out to the full in the belief that something
> hidden there will manifest itself to us.
>
> —Henri Nouwen

Introduction

Let's face it. Waiting is hard, especially in a culture when everything is promised in an instant: fast food, instant pudding, precooked dinners, real-time feedback, immediate weight loss, on demand viewing, speed dating, drive-thru counseling, two-hour grocery delivery, a four-year college degree in less than two years, even fluency in a foreign language over the weekend! We don't want to wait, we don't like to wait, and we're not very good at it. For most of us, patience is not in our top skill set. Sadly, impatience is a learned disability. No one I know lists patience or the ability to wait on their resumes as prime proficiencies when seeking a new job or elective office. We are good at planning, at doing, at action, at accomplishing—but waiting, being patient? Not so much.

Yet, for Paul, patience is the first practice on the list for a congregation in turmoil, and for us, too. In this chapter, we'll examine together what it means to be willing to stay where we are and practice patience. As we will see, patience means more than just showing up from time to time, hoping that things have changed. Rather, it demands full engagement—living the situation to the full, and this is rarely easy. Patience provides time for all of us to pay attention, to look for things that are hidden in our midst and that will, in good time—in holy time, manifest themselves. Thus, patience is ultimately an act of faith in a God who is with us and who is working in the messes we face and make, bringing hope and healing as we learn to love each other, perhaps the hardest thing we will ever be asked to do. Love, if it is anything, is patient.

A Conversation About Patience

Before we look more closely at three aspects of patience that can be practiced in our faith communities (remember that the Apostle Paul wrote 1 Corinthians 13 to a group of Christians whose congregation was in a mess), let me share a conversation I had with my parents as they shared the frustrations and the virtues of worshiping in the same small church for over fifty years. Hopefully, it will be easy to connect the dots, a task I leave to you.

Staying at the Same Church for a Very Long Time

When my parents came to visit my wife and me in San Diego one February from their home in central Michigan, we had a chance to talk with them over dinner about their lives together, living in the same small house, in the same small town, and attending the same small church for over fifty-five years. "Did you ever get bored?" I asked. "Oh, no," my mother replied, "between sports, scouting, school, church activities, meals, laundry, and driving the school bus, I could hardly manage each day. Remember, we didn't have all that stuff like video games or microwaves or computers or GPS or smart phones back then. We had to make our way all on our own." It wasn't the first time that I had heard that observation.

I do remember that our family life was rich and full. Indeed, I had a happy childhood and I have many fond memories of our church activities, too, really the centerpiece of our lives. I wondered out loud, however, if staying in the same small church for more than fifty years might have had some drawbacks. After a moment of reflection, my mother began: "Well, we did have one pastor who couldn't preach worth a lick, so he tried to make up for it by being long-winded. That didn't work, and he moved on after three years or so. And there were some who wanted more preaching each week about creation or the end times, but I didn't see much sense in debating about it since no one was going to change their mind anyway. Me, I don't think that there were any witnesses at the creation, and I'm a pan-millennialist. I believe it will all pan out in the end," she said with a smile. It wasn't the first time that I had heard that one either.

At that point, my dad leaned in and added, "The music wasn't always the best. We had a couple who sat in the back row of our pews each Sunday and plugged their ears with their fingers because they thought the organ was too loud. And one Christmas, a young boy played a drum solo—"Little Drummer Boy." And I mean a drum solo—he had a single snare drum and he beat it as best he could all by himself. No accompaniment of any kind. The only way we knew the song was done was when he stopped drumming, put his drumsticks in his pocket, and walked off the platform and back to his seat. We all clapped to provide a little encouragement and recognition for his efforts, but it wasn't all that good really. And it was difficult to muster enough regulars for a choir, but we did have several who could really sing. We looked forward when it was their turn to bring a special before the pastor came to preach."

I asked them why they didn't think about attending another church, a bigger church with more resources and programs. "Oh, to be honest we did once or twice, but in the end, this was our church and these were our people. This is where we met, this is where we were married, this is where all the boys were dedicated to the Lord, this was where our family was established, and this is where we buried our parents. And this is where we walked with our friends when they did the same—through good and terrible times, and there were some of both. We stood with them and walked with them, and they walked with us on our journey. What more could you ask for?" Mother said as she wiped some tears from her eyes and Dad blew his nose with his big red handkerchief. And to bring the conversation to a close, she added, "We stayed because we believed that God was at work in us and through us, and we believed that the goodness of God would come our way, but it wasn't going to come on our timing. And when tough times showed up, where else would you want to be than with your people, people who knew you and loved you anyway? In the end, we received far more than we ever gave. That's the way church works if you stick with it and make it part of your life."

When Paul told the Corinthians that love is patient, I think he was saying much the same thing.

Willing to Stay Where We Are

Patience is the ability to endure difficult circumstances—such as perseverance in the face of delay, tolerance of provocation without responding in annoyance/anger, or forbearance when under strain, especially when faced with long-term difficulties. Patience is also the level of endurance one can have before negativity sets in. To endure, persevere, tolerate, and forbear—these are the actions associated with patience. Such words do not make us want to do the happy dance. In fact, they suggest some sort of struggle. Indeed, the Apostle Paul points out in his letter to the Romans that suffering brings the necessity to persevere, perseverance in turn builds character, and with character comes hope (5:3–4). Hope I'll take; but suffering and perseverance that builds that kind of character, not so much.

Yet, there it is. Staying and waiting are difficult but formative spiritual practices. Tolstoy saw time and patience as the two great warriors of life, and my father was fond of saying that time heals all wounds and wounds all heels. I think they are both probably right, but that doesn't make it any easier to stay and wait, even if we know that good can come from it. When my father responded to my complaining about how tough things were by saying, "It builds character," he was probably right again, but let's be honest, most things that build that kind of character are no picnic.

And this is particularly true when we find ourselves in a dysfunctional church situation. In fact, waiting and staying are the last things we want to think about, and it is the last thing that many of us would ever do. For most of us, including me, a more honest response is, "I'm outta here!" And if truth be told, there are plenty of other congregations ready and excited to take you in. In fact, the lifeblood of many congregations is the constant migration of professing Christians from one church to another—a migration that would put the Serengeti to shame. As one pastor told me, "Some will come and some will go. That's just the way it is. No use paying any attention to who they are or why they go. Once they're gone, they're gone. We have to focus on intake." And at a conference on spiritual disciplines, I heard a speaker say that the church is pretty good at getting folk across the border into a new land, but not so good at helping them move to the interior and make a new home, one with deep roots and formative relationships. Sadly, most of our efforts are designed for intake, for those who are shopping, dating, or simply on a test drive. Clearly, the church is better at sales and marketing than at production and formation.

Yet Paul tells us that the very heart and soul of love (even in a dysfunctional congregation—perhaps especially in a dysfunctional congregation) is patience and kindness, and patience is the first practice he mentions. This is not the kind of patience we exhibit when we are waiting for Christmas or a promotion or an online order to arrive. No, the patient love that Paul is referring to is long-suffering, and in a dysfunctional congregation, you will find a good deal of suffering all around you, and it will find you, too. You can count on it, yet if I understand Paul correctly, this is what we're called to do and where we're called to be—to practice patience in the middle of the mess, to be patient in the middle of the mess. So, how do we survive without being overwhelmed by it all? The key, I think, is found in the epigraph at the beginning of this chapter (Henri Nouwen). We need to be willing to stay, committed to leaning in and living out the situation to the full. Of course, this is much easier said than done, so we'll try to make some sense of it in the next section. Suffice it here to say, we are called to practice active patience, and that requires much more from us than just showing up when we're in the mood for a good song and a free cup of coffee. We need to stay with spiritual intent.

Living the Situation Out to the Full

There are different ways of waiting, of course, and there is a huge difference between just showing up and being fully in. I believe that we are called to be engaged, not just present each Sunday. It's not just an attendance contest. I am reminded of a decision point I reached during the spring of my high school senior year. It was track season and I ran the half-mile and anchored the mile relay. It was also right after a very good basketball season where we went deep in the state tournament. To be honest, I loved playing basketball far more than working out on the track, so several of us went to the gym and played basketball instead of stretching and participating in the first half of our designated workouts. Of course, when the track coach found out what we were doing, he locked the gym and instructed us to be present for the entire track practice, which makes perfect sense to me now, but at the time it felt like a major uninvited intrusion into my day.

I remember sitting on the riverbank near the running track when the head coach came over and asked me what I was doing. "I guess I'm pouting," I said with a half-smile, "trying to decide if I should quit running and just play basketball after school." "Well," he began slowly and softly, "that's your choice, of course, but please consider this for a minute. You can play pickup basketball games anytime you want for the rest of your life, but this is the only opportunity you will ever have to run track in high school with this team. And you're a leader. What you do will influence others, too. They are watching to see how you respond, so this decision is bigger than you know. Still, it is up to you." At that point, the coach looked me squarely in the eyes and said, "But know this. If you are going to run track, you have to be willingly all in. I don't just want your legs; I need your spirit, too. A half-hearted runner will infect the entire team, so it's all in or go home. Got that?"

I got it. I showed up for practice every day—all in, and I'm glad I did. Looking back, I would have missed out on so many good times that created lifelong memories and unexpected friendships. And the icing on the cake was that I usually found time in the evenings to shoot hoops in the driveway at home, too, albeit with tired legs, and that actually made me a better basketball player. I learned how to deal with fatigue and adjust my shot accordingly, something that paid dividends throughout my college basketball career.

Willingly all in. That was the key. And I think that it is applicable to church attendance, too. Even when we stay, there are different ways of staying. Some helpful, some not so much. There is the half-hearted, "I don't want to get involved" approach—"I'll come most Sundays, but please don't ask me to do anything. I'm here, but my spirit is shooting hoops in the gym or thinking about a trip to the beach." There's the "I'm wearing a mask" approach—"I'm here but don't expect me to connect in any honest way. I have a plastic smile and I like the way I look." There's the "protection" approach—"I've been hurt before, so I'm in full armor. I won't let anyone get close to me, and I'll lash out at the drop of a hat." And, of course, there's the "bitter wait" approach—"I'm hurt but I'm here, hoping to see this church implode. What goes around will come around—and I can't wait to see others get what they deserve."

Of course, there are other ways of staying that are not helpful to anyone, but I think you get the point. We can stay and not be willingly all in, and we pay a price for doing so. Others are infected, too. When Henri Nouwen wrote about the willingness to stay where we are *and* live the situation out to the full, I believe that he was saying much the same thing.

So, how do we stay engaged in our community of faith willingly all in—living the situation out to the full? The first key is to show up every week, whether you want to or not. Consider it a spiritual practice, one that will shape and form you in ways known and unknown. You can't practice presence from a distance.

And be mindful that we are all wounded in one way or another—we're all broken pots. When I complained to my boss that there seemed to be a good deal of ignorance arriving at the university with each new freshman class, he reminded me that if you run a hospital, you shouldn't be surprised when sick people show up. He was right, of course, and I got his point. If we are to walk with those who claim Christ and with those who don't, the wounded will be present because that is all of us. It is the soil in which the seeds of grace and healing take root and grow.

It is also important to maintain a healthy compassion orbit. Think about a satellite circling the earth. If it gets too close to the earth, gravity will pull it in, causing it to crash and burn. However, if the orbit is too far away from earth, the satellite will simply drift off, out of touch and unable to function as it was intended. I believe the same holds true for our presence in the church. If our compassion orbit is too low, we end up being pulled into every drama or jumping in to solve and save every problem in the church. And when we do, we crash and burn. On the other hand, it is not helpful for us or anyone else for that matter to be so distant that we simply drift off, out of touch, unable or unwilling to lean in and serve where needed. It seems to me the key is to maintain a healthy compassion orbit, close enough to recognize a need that we can address, and yet distant enough that we recognize that none of us are called to save the entire circus. I acknowledge that maintaining healthy boundaries can be a difficult task when so much needs to be done, so it is helpful to have a friend or two who knows you well enough to watch your orbit and honest enough to tell you when you are off course.

One final comment about staying and staying engaged: it's not always a picnic in the park. In fact, it rarely is. Aristotle said that while the fruit of patience is sweet, patience itself can be quite bitter. I guess that's where the word *long-suffering* comes into play. To be honest, showing up each week, leaning in, and serving behind the scenes without receiving any recognition and expression of gratitude will test our spirits, but if we make it about us, it will kill them. So, are we to just put up with all of this as best we can? Where does our faith come into play, if it comes into play at all? And is God at work, or are we doing a solo act with all the heavy lifting? These are honest and earnest questions, of course, but as we will see in what follows, the key is to maintain a faithful perspective, to look to the horizon with eyes of faith, something that is not always easy in a church culture where our attendance is based on much the same set of criteria that we use to select a playground for our kids or a good place to have a picnic.

Believing That Something Hidden Will Manifest Itself

The good news is that God is always present, at work long before we show up and will be at work long after we are gone. So even when it looks like nothing is happening, something *is* happening. The key is to believe—to know that something hidden will manifest itself. That makes our work, all of it, sacred, even when it is church work, perhaps especially so. Staying and leaning in may be the most potent prayer we will ever pray, particularly when we do so as an expression of our faith in a God who is present and at work, too.

In essence, we are expressing a faith in what is not yet seen, and in what we may not see in our lifetime. There are no guarantees. The great faith chapter in Hebrews lists five faithful pilgrims—Abel, Enoch, Noah, Abraham, and Sarah (11:4–12), and adds that while they were still living by faith when they died, they didn't receive the things that were promised to them. Instead, they only saw and welcomed them from a distance (13a)—through the eyes of faith, believing that something would manifest itself in due time.

When we stay and lean in, believing that God is at work and that something will manifest itself in divine time, we are invited into the spiritual practice of paying attention to the little signs and signals that grace *is* at work among us, through us, and in us, too. We stay and wait with feet firmly planted and eyes fixed on the horizon, looking for the evidence of things not yet seen. It is not always easy, but it is good. We practice presence because love is patient.

Scripture

In each chapter, there is a section where we turn to the Scriptures for insight and instruction. Hopefully, I will offer some helpful commentary and not just snatch a verse or two and use them totally out of context to buttress my own beliefs and opinions, an all-too-common practice known as prooftexting—even though the temptation is always great. I read the Bible most days, and I try to do so carefully, prayerfully, and faithfully, but I am mindful that we, all of us, bring our own filters and experiences when attempting to read and understand any text, including sacred ones—perhaps especially those that are sacred to us. This places a huge obligation on me to be as fair to the text as I can be—an obligation I take seriously, and it places an obligation on each reader to read thoughtfully and carefully with spiritual eyes wide open, allowing the Holy Spirit to be the truth-guide. Needless to say, but I'll say it anyway—there is a Holy Spirit, and it is not me. Please keep that in mind when you read my reflections on Scripture—or anyone else's for that matter. Perspective is important.

The God of the Patient Wait

It's difficult to understand God's timing, let alone predict it. When we look back, it is often easy to see God's fingerprints all over our lives, but not so when looking to the future or when looking around. What is clear to me is that our God is the God of the Patient Wait. You can turn to almost any place in the Bible, and there you will find God patiently waiting for something or another, and humans impatiently waiting and wondering if they have been abandoned. God took six days to create our world. I suppose he could have done so with a wink of an eye and a few magic words, but not so. And after six days, God rested, although I'm sure that there were many other tasks to attend to (Gen 1:1–2:3). God is a patient creator.

God patiently waited until there was only one righteous family left on earth before unleashing the skies that led to a great flood, and then promised to never do it again (Gen 6–9). And God was willing to negotiate with Abraham on behalf of Sodom if he could find fifty righteous men—no, forty-five, no, forty, thirty-five, thirty, twenty-five, twenty, fifteen, even ten! In the end, Abraham could not find even ten, but I can't help wondering if God would have been willing to patiently negotiate even further. Obviously, he was in no hurry to give them what they deserved. We can all be thankful for such mercy.

And the list could go on and on—years in bondage in Egypt, years wandering in the desert, years in exile (more than once), years with an erratic king, years under siege, and years waiting for the Messiah to come, to name just a few. Of course, there were good years, too, but even then, there was a sense of waiting—that something was coming, and it was coming on God's own time, not ours.

Speaking of God's own timing, we often think of the Apostle Paul's Damascus Road experience as three days that transformed Paul's vision and immediately catapulted him on to his missionary journeys. Surely, that experience did change Paul, but there is much more to the story. After a visit from Jesus on the way to Damascus (Acts: 9), Paul left and headed south into the Arabian Desert on a pilgrimage, tracing the route taken by one of his heroes, Elijah (1 Kgs 19). After a time, perhaps as much as three years, he returned to Jerusalem and presented himself to Peter and James, the leaders of the budding but oppressed Christian church. After a very brief preaching stint in the local synagogues, Paul was escorted down to Caesarea and put on a boat back to Tarsus, his hometown. He stayed in Tarsus for almost a decade before Barnabas showed up and accompanied him to Antioch where Paul began his missionary efforts in earnest (Acts 9–11). Even after one of the most life-changing encounters with Jesus ever recorded, Paul had to patiently wait and prepare for his public ministry. God is the God of the Patient Wait—even for apostles.

Perhaps the best illustration of God's patience for us can be found in the parable of the Prodigal Son (Luke 15:11–32). The impetuous younger son did not want to wait for his inheritance, and even though the father knew that it would be a disaster, he gave his son his share, which he immediately went out and squandered, finally leading to a job tending and eating with the pigs—not the destination he had envisioned and not an occupation for any self-respecting Jew. And what was the father doing during all this time? He was patiently waiting for any sign of his son's silhouette on the horizon, for *any* sign that he wanted to come home, and as soon as he caught a tiny glimpse of movement a long ways away, he took off on a dead sprint to welcome him home and throw a party in his honor.

There is plenty of good news in this parable for all of us, because we are prodigals, too, impatient and bull-headed, thinking we know better and wanting what we want right now! Over and over again, God has proven to be loving enough to give us freedom, even when we don't know where we're going or what we are going to do when we get there, and patient enough to wait until we make even the slightest move toward home. When we do, grace comes running and the celebrations begin, which is far more than we could ever imagine or deserve. I pray that we can all practice this kind of patience with each other, especially with those in our own faith community. When we do, we honor our God of the Patient Wait.

Some Next Steps

Let me offer a few words of practical advice about being patient. It is easier for most of us to meditate and ruminate about things than it is to take some concrete steps to address them. When I taught management, I was fond of saying that good intentions without timely execution is a form of self-deception. My dad would say that some talkers he knew had big hats but no cattle. I think we were mostly saying the same thing—talk without action is cheap. So, if we are serious about exercising patience, what are some practical next steps? Let me offer three.

Clarify Your Expectations for Church

A good first step is to identify and examine your motives for going to church in the first place. Given its context, resources, and mission, what can you reasonably expect from your faith community? What *do* you expect from your faith community? What do you hope to receive and what do you intend to give? Do you expect to be involved in any meaningful way? Obviously, your church should occupy a central place in your life, but it was never intended to be an entertainment establishment or a social club or a daycare facility. It was never intended to replace or exclude family, friends, and community engagement. Honestly, if you come to church thinking that it was designed solely for you and with all your particular needs in mind, you will quickly become dissatisfied—and disillusioned, too. Be clear about your expectations for church, and carefully and prayerfully examine them in light of the true mission of the church. Perspective will encourage perseverance.

HALT!

HALT has become a mainstay in many addiction programs, and it has been adopted and adapted for many other kinds of organizations and efforts as well. HALT stands for hungry, angry, lonely, and tired—and it serves as a reminder that when our physical or emotional or spiritual needs are not met, it puts us in a deficit condition and poor decisions are often the result. The original idea was that if you are hungry, angry, lonely, or tired, you need to be very careful because relapse is likely under these conditions. Today, many leadership and management consultants use HALT to suggest that these conditions often lead to poor organizational decisions for leaders and unfortunate individual choices for all of us who try to follow.

What I have found to be true is that when we are in HALT mode, it is extremely difficult to be patient—with church, with others, and with ourselves, too. When the inclination to leave church arises, and it will for most of us at one time or another, it is good to first take stock of your life and your lifestyle to be sure that you are not in HALT mode. If you are, then it is important to address these physical and emotional deficits before any important decisions are made about church.

Keep in Step with the Spirit

We read in Galatians 5:25, "Since we live by the Spirit, let us keep in step with the Spirit." Here I believe that Paul is telling us something very important—don't just stand there, walk! And as you do, watch where you're walking, be open to new paths or avenues of service and growth, and embrace the mystery of God's timing and your own fears and doubts, too—trust anyway. Keep moving, but how?

A good place to start moving is with some daily spiritual practices. Let me mention just two: (1) bookending your day and (2) acknowledging God's presence in the everyday life. These practices are not earthshaking, but they will shape and form you if you take them seriously and practice them regularly. By bookending, I mean starting each day with intention and ending each day with gratitude. Take some quiet time early each day to pray—with an emphasis on listening rather than talking. Ask God to show you how to keep step with the Spirit that particular day, your today, and to be mindful of God's leading. Start with intention, and then end your day with gratitude by sharing with someone (or journaling or blogging) when you felt closest to God that day and when you saw the Spirit at work. This bookending practice invites all of us to start the day with a focus on God's work in us and through us and ends with a recognition that God has been faithful. It is a simple but powerful daily spiritual practice.

Another spiritual practice that complements bookending is the simple Ignatian custom of acknowledging that God is always present by simply repeating, "God is present," regardless of what you are facing at the time, whether it be good, bad, or ugly. In the midst of an argument with a loved one, or hearing the test results from a biopsy, or filling up your car with gas, or taking a walk in the neighborhood, things take on a deeper spiritual meaning when you recognize God's presence.

And this is particularly true when we find ourselves waiting—perhaps especially so in waiting. Paul tells us that love is patient, and we realize that exercising this kind of love often requires waiting, even long-suffering. At the end of the day, however, such waiting will change us if we keep in step with the Spirit and live true to the reality that God is always present and at work—in us, through us, and for us, too.

* * *

Exemptions: Time to Go

Before we close this chapter on patience and waiting, I want to acknowledge that there are conditions where we are not obligated to stay—in fact, we shouldn't stay. We must leave. Church is hard for many of us at one time or another, so we have to learn new skills to swim upstream. Swimming upstream can make you tired, so you have to be intentional about self-care when you do; but swimming up a toxic stream will make you sick. If you find yourself in a toxic stream, it's time to get out, let go, and move on. Let me give three all too familiar examples.

Abusive or Venomous Relationships

The first toxic example is being unable to avoid an abusive or venomous relationship. The most hopeful strategy is to find reconciliation, of course, or at least so limit any contact that this relationship does not affect your work or your ability to worship. But let's be painfully honest, sometimes there is no way to minimize contact. This relationship undermines all you are trying to do and the kind of person that you are trying to be. In a perfect world, we'd all attend a Truth and Reconciliation Commission meeting, and all would be forgiven—but honestly, it doesn't always work like that, even when we do all we can. In the face of an abusive or venomous relationship, being patient does not require you to stay. Time to go.

Authoritarian or Narcissistic Leadership

The second toxic stream to avoid is authoritarian or narcissistic leadership. There are many effective leadership styles, but after years of teaching leadership, I am convinced that any organization that requires strict adherence to anything the leadership deems appropriate and delegitimizes and stifles all honest questions and expressions of concern is, at best, dangerous. And it is important to look carefully at how the church community draws the line between "us and them." It is a big red flag when new members are told that they must be totally in or get out (without any engagement or discernment)—and particularly so when it is on the organization's own terms, which it usually is. When a church insists that it has all the truth and understanding and it is up to you to buy in and fall in line or leave, I would suggest the latter.

A second form of toxic leadership is narcissism. Now I admit that it takes a strong ego to lead any effort, and certainly a religious organization where no one has to show up on any given Sunday, most of your help is from volunteers, and everyone feels free to offer their criticisms and suggestions for improvement on a regular basis. I get that, but when the leader is self-centered, self-absorbed, vain, conceited, and convinced of his or her own importance, there is trouble brewing. Honestly, I have to admit that some narcissistic leaders command organizations that look solid from the outside, at least in the short run, but such leadership ultimately breeds unhealthy competition, unwanted conflict, and unnecessary hurt—especially for staff and key volunteers. Good things are happening, but at a great and unnecessary personal cost to many. When the agenda for the organization is all about the leader and not the mission, it's time to go.

Damaging or Misguided Theology

When it comes to theology, churches are all over the road. Some promote a "big tent" approach, embracing various ideas and theologies with a sense of welcome and hospitality, and others are very restrictive, exclusive even. There must be a fundamental affirmation in your spirit that what the church advocates about important things is acceptable—the reading and interpretation of Scripture, the divinity of Christ, the role of women in ministry, the validity of the sacraments, and who is welcome—to name just a few. I am not advocating any particular theological point of view here, but I am arguing that you can't be "all in" with your community of faith if you have deep and honest disagreement and concerns with the central tenets espoused publicly or held privately. If it isn't a good fit, you will feel it, and over time it will fester. Better to find a faith fellowship where you are given enough theological space to feel at home.

Seasons of Life

In no way do I want to discount the working and leading of the Holy Spirit. There are seasons in all of our lives where we sense the Spirit's leading, and sometimes it is to leave and embark on a spiritual journey, even if like Abraham we don't know where we are going (Heb 11:8). We may sense that our work is done in a certain place or assignment and a new season is about to unfold. When this is the case, the leading of the Holy Spirit trumps even the words of Paul bidding us to be patient and stay. It is important, of course, to have a trusted friend or spiritual director with whom you can discuss this tug of the heart, since we can be misguided or impatient. We know that God is the God of the Patient Wait, so it is prudent to take plenty of time and be discerning before making a major move. As the old Quaker saying goes—Way will open in front of you and Way will close behind you.

Conclusion

In our culture, *patience* isn't a happy word, and in the church world bent toward being seeker-sensitive, we shop for a place to worship like we shop for a new car. In fact, we are encouraged to do so. Of course, church can be hard, and it is for most of us at one time or another. The Apostle Paul was writing to a church in a big mess in 1 Corinthians, too, and his message was to be patient and be kind. Honestly, that's a tall order.

We took to heart the encouragement from Henri Nouwen in the epigraph of this chapter that patience means the willingness to stay where we are and to be all in, believing and expecting that something hidden will manifest—but in the Spirit's own timing, not ours. We looked to Scripture, seeing time after time where God was the God of the Patient Wait, and took heart in the story of the Prodigal Son, noting that with even the slightest turn toward home, the Father will come running. We then examined two spiritual practices that can fill our cups in the midst of waiting: bookending our days and acknowledging the presence of God in even our most ordinary activities.

Even in a chapter dedicated to patience and waiting, we noted that there are toxic situations that are exemptions to the long-suffering rule: abusive and venomous relationships that cannot be negotiated, authoritarian and narcissistic leadership that demand adherence without allowing for questions and concerns to be expressed, and damaging and misguided theologies that claim to hold all truth and exclude all other points of view. Such conditions will not only make you tired—they will also make you sick. Under such conditions, it's time to go.

Finally, we acknowledged that there are seasons of life for all of us, and sometimes we sense the Spirit's leading to leave. When we do, we follow, even if like Abraham we don't know exactly where we are going. So, there are exemptions to the rule, but the intent is clear. When church life gets messy, and it either is or will be for most of us, the first inclination is to run, but Paul calls us to wait patiently for the work of God to manifest itself in due time—God's time. At the end of the day, the promise is that it will.

Questions for Reflection and Discussion:

1. Looking back, have you ever left a church situation that you now regret in some way? That is, have you ever left a faith community for the wrong reasons or poorly? Explain.

2. Have you ever stayed at a church, but for the wrong reasons—and with a bad attitude? How did that work out?

3. How would it change your day if you started with the intention of seeing God at work and desiring to participate in it, and ended each day in gratitude for the opportunities that came your way?

4. Do you feel that you are in a toxic situation that is making you sick, yet you are reluctant to move on, perhaps feeling that if you did so, you would be simply running away or seen as a failure? Do you have a friend, mentor, or spiritual director that you could talk to about all of this, and if not, where might you find one?

5. Do you have any stories that you could share about times when you or someone you know waited patiently, all in, and something good did manifest itself? Such stories serve as an encouragement to all of us.

Love is patient . . .

— 2 —

Love Is Kind

The simplest acts of kindness are by far more powerful than a thousand heads bowing in prayer.

—Mahatma Gandhi

Introduction

It started out as an ordinary lunch with my good friend at our favorite German restaurant in San Diego, but unexpectedly our conversation took on a serious tone—it went deep. I mentioned something about wondering how we were going to be remembered someday, and it must have struck a tender chord. He leaned in, cleared his throat, and began to share in almost a whisper that some years ago, his marriage was on the rocks, truly hanging by a thread, so they made a last-ditch effort to salvage the relationship by seeing a marriage counselor. In their first session, they both admitted that the marriage was over, that whatever they had once was gone. The counselor granted that much had been lost but asked about the things that they remembered seeing in each other as they fell in love and married. He began by sharing some of the things he saw in his wife when they first met, and certainly there was much that attracted him to her. Then it was his wife's turn. After a long and awkward silence, she said that the only thing she could think of was that he was kind. That was it.

Now it was our turn in the conversation to sit in silence. Finally, he looked at me and said, "Kind—that's it. Can you believe it? I was hoping for smart, bold, outgoing, positive, generous, handsome, and fun. Maybe sexy, too, but all I got was kind. It really hurt, and I've carried it with me to this day. Somehow, it made me feel terribly inadequate. Kind. He is K-I-N-D! Are you kidding me!"

"Look," I said, wanting to give him a hug—but hugging wasn't in our repertoire of interactions, "I'm sure there was no intent to hurt you. In the midst of a very difficult and dark time, words are hard to find and often surface clumsily. You certainly have many redeeming qualities, but honestly, the more I think about it, if someone were to summarize my life and chose kindness as its expression, I'd say that my life was a success. Indeed, if sometime in the future—granted, hopefully a long way into the future—someone wrote about me, *He was kind*, I would be satisfied, holding that as the highest compliment anyone could give. At the end of the day, being kind is the most Christian way I know to live."

When the Apostle Paul wrote that love is kind, I think he was saying much the same thing. In this chapter, we'll look a bit closer at kindness, speculating about why Paul brought kindness to the fore when we face a messy church situation instead of a number of other virtues that he could have highlighted, and why patience and kindness are so intertwined. We'll also examine how the practice of kindness is described today and why it is so rare, and what we can do if we desire to be a kinder person. As we will see, there is no kindness switch that we can just turn on. In fact, I don't believe that we can just decide one day to be kind, but we can with patience and resolve choose to be kinder. Kindness is a long journey, and when our faith community is in turmoil, it will take the very grace of God to pull it off. Thankfully, grace does abound.

Kindness

For a church in a mess, why did the Apostle Paul start with patience and kindness rather than prayer and Bible reading? I suppose that he may have just assumed that the congregation would be praying and reading the Scriptures (remember, however, that much of what is now the New Testament had not yet been written), but I think the reason goes much deeper than that. At a recent conference on a Christian response to addictions of all sorts, the keynote speaker, a pastor and trained clinician, started out by saying that the most common Christian response to those with addictions is to tell them that they should pray harder and read the Bible more each day. This approach, according to the speaker was, indeed, sad, and sadly insufficient. While there is much to be gained through prayer and Bible study, there is rarely a "presto" moment when the addictions are simply and completely eradicated. Rather, it is a long, hard, and complex growth process that takes sustained effort and constant support. Honestly, I think the same advice is appropriate for a church in a mess. Of course, prayer and Bible study are helpful, but patience and kindness are essential, too, perhaps even more so. When Gandhi wrote that the simplest acts of kindness are far more powerful than a thousand heads bowing in prayer, I believe this is exactly what he was getting at. He wasn't demeaning the power of prayer, but rather giving it wings.

Kindness emerges from within. It is a state of being—a kind of presence, a quality of life that emerges from a certain embrace of the world. Kindness has been described as a childlike faith in God and the ability to extend the benefit of the doubt—not only to others, but to God and to ourselves, too. No doubt, such an approach to life is risky, taking deep humility and a sincere faith in the consistent goodness of God, but I have come to believe that kindness is one of the most potent spiritual practices available to us as Christians, and perhaps the single most healing balm available to a faith community in crisis. The Holy Spirit works through the extension of kindness.

Why is kindness so powerful? Let me give three reasons. First, acts of kindness move our spirits, right where we live, all the way to our toes. A simple act of kindness can change the entire trajectory of a person's life. It warms the heart, communicates safety, and enables honest relationships, and unexpected acts of kindness, while costing practically nothing, can be the most profound gift we can offer or receive. In short, kindness takes all of us by surprise, and there is no downside.

Second, kindness is never wasted. In fact, it multiplies. It has a ripple effect, even if we do not know where the impact will ultimately be felt, and it moves out in many directions, like the roots that shoot out from a plant, producing more of the same in the most unlikely and unpredicted places. Thus, there is no such thing as a simple act of kindness because each act has its own spiritual trajectory. We simply act kindly and let the Holy Spirit do the heavy lifting.

Finally, kindness is the soil in which other virtues are sustained. It is difficult, for example, to think of generosity, compassion, or mercy without kindness at their core. We give, care, and forgive as expressions of kindness—of that which has been extended to us. In short, kindness is so powerful because it hits us right where we live, it has an unpredictable and unexplainable way of multiplying itself, and it fosters the growth and exercise of other communal virtues as well. It is grace at work.

A fair question to ask is this: if kindness is so powerful, why is it so rarely practiced—especially in a messy church situation? Fair question, indeed. As a start, kindness can be seen as weakness, and to be honest, people can and will from time to time take advantage of our willingness to give the benefit of the doubt. I get that, but that's on them, isn't it? We are called to be faithful. If someone twists our good intentions, all we can do is stay the course. While it is true that what goes around often comes around, that is not up to us. We're called to be the lovers, and as Paul put it—love is kind.

I think it is also fair to say that kindness is rare in our culture because it is not a "resume virtue." When we build our resumes, we list our goals, strengths, activities, and accomplishments, but there is no place for qualities like kindness and patience. It's about performance, talents, and accomplishments. It isn't until we build our vitae or someone builds it for us (the things they say about us at our memorial service or the grave site) that kindness comes into play. When others look back on our lives, who wants to be remembered for running a good committee meeting (as rare as that talent is)? Rather, if they say *she was kind*, that just about says it all. At the end of the day or at the end of our days, kindness carries the day.

So, can we just decide to be kind? Probably not, but we can choose to be kinder. Kindness is a choice we make about how we will walk in this world each day. It begins with the understanding that we all struggle, all of us—we're broken pots, and with the recognition that we are all fighting a battle of one kind or another. When this finally sinks in, it allows—no, demands—that we extend kindness without any conditions. In first grade, I slipped a note to Julie at recess that read: I'll like you *if* you like me. *If* was the operative word. And it is the operative word in our church world, too. I will like you *if* you like me or I'll be friendly to you *if* you start being more friendly, or I'll be kind *if* . . . When it comes down to it, there's no *if* in kindness. We just choose to be kinder anyway, each day, every day, even when it seems that there isn't a way forward. In some deeply spiritual sense, we become kind as we choose to make kindness a daily discipline.

Acts of kindness shape and form us in the image of the Christ we wish to follow—even when life, including our church, is messy, perhaps especially when we're in a mess. On Paul's account, patience and kindness go together, like two sides of the same coin. Patience gives kindness a long life, and kindness gives patience potency and purpose. Certainly, they enrich each other as they enrich our lives when they are faithfully practiced. It is love at its best.

Scripture

I spent a week each summer with my grandparents, and I loved it. Perhaps the fact that they lived on a beautiful lake had something to do with it, and perhaps the fact that I could go with my grandfather each morning and work in the Allen Lumber Company Office had something to do with it, too, but my fondest memories have to do with our morning devotions. After the breakfast dishes with cleared away, we would go into the living room and take a seat. First, my grandmother would read from the Bible and we would sing a hymn. Then we all knelt by our chairs. My grandfather would pray out loud—with passion! Before the devotional time was over, we all took our turn at praying. When I prayed, I mustered as much passion as I could.

Just before we headed out the door for work, I would stop by my grandmother's hutch. On the middle shelf was a ceramic loaf of bread with about seventy or so little cards protruding from the top. On the side of the loaf were the words—*Our Daily Bread*. Each little card contained a promise from Scripture. I guess the idea was that you would pull one out at random and that would be your promise for the day. However, sometimes I didn't particularly like the promise I drew from the loaf of bread or it didn't seem to be relevant, so I quickly put the promise back into the loaf and drew another. Sometimes, I did so more than once until I "received" the perfect promise from the Lord.

In the section that follows, we will look at five verses from Proverbs that speak about being kind. To be honest, some verses are more difficult to understand and discuss, so I was tempted to put two of them back in the daily bread loaf. In the end, however, I believe all five have something to say to us today as they, and we, are all connected in a deep spiritual way.

The Benefits of Kindness

"Those who are kind benefit themselves, but the cruel bring ruin on themselves" (Prov 11:17). On the face of it, there are at least two ideas here that do not always ring true. For one thing, I have watched those who extend kindness at one time or another be taken advantage of by the recipients of that kindness. Indeed, some have cautioned that it is not always good to be kind because others will see you as naïve or weak and play you for the fool. It does happen. It has happened to me.

The second idea—that the cruel bring ruin on themselves—also rings a bit hollow. I have witnessed and experienced cruel treatment that did not lead to ruin. In fact, such behavior was ignored and even rewarded as long as giving increased and the numbers trended upward. In too many cases, board members turn a blind eye to cruel and self-serving behaviors as long as the "business metrics" of the church are met and no one brings legal action.

So, given this sad experience, is it possible that there is a benefit to kind behavior, even if others take advantage of the kindness? And do cruel persons really hurt themselves, even if it appears that they are rewarded for their hurtful actions? For me, the answer is a resounding *Yes*! How can this be? First, remember that kind behavior shapes the giver, no matter if it is accepted or how it is viewed or abused. Kind behavior benefits the giver because it both reflects the image of Christ and forms the giver in good ways. How an extended kindness is received is up to the receiver—it's on them. Our job is simply to be the lover, and as Paul tells us, love is kind.

And regardless of how cruelty is rewarded, it diminishes that person whether they recognize it or not. At the end of the day, we all have to look in the mirror and face the way we have conducted our lives. Even if our resumes report success after success, it means very little if our vita, our life, is silent. When others look back on our lives, it would be very sad if nothing good could be said about us other than the fact that we were punctual at work and drove a nice car. In my view, that would be ruin.

Encouragement

"Anxiety weighs down the heart, but a kind word cheers it up" (Prov 12:25). We've heard it said in so many ways, but the truth of the matter is simply this: anxiety and worry weigh down the spirit. They sap the heart. I watched a young mother take her son who was acting up outside the church one Sunday morning for a "parental conversation." They sat on a bench and the boy was crying, kicking his feet, clenching his fist, and pounding on the bench as his mother whispered sternly in his ear. It was painful to watch, and since the entire front of the church was glass, it must have been public and painful for them, too. As they were preparing to return to the sanctuary, I felt a nudge to speak to the mother. Honestly, I don't know why the nudge came to me and I wasn't sure what to say, but I walked over to the mother and softly whispered, "You are a good mother." That's all I knew to say. She looked at me and her tears immediately started to flow. She told my wife later that she was feeling like a horrible mother—a total failure. She was at wit's end, and my words were a comfort to her during another episode of a trying season.

Simple acts of kindness are a form of encouragement, and while encouragement costs nothing, it means everything when our hearts are heavy. It won't immediately solve all the problems we face, but encouragement has a spiritual power that, while difficult to quantify, is powerful, nonetheless. Sadly, when a church is in a mess, kind words are seldom offered or acknowledged, yet they may well be the path to healing and hope. I believe that the Holy Spirit works through kindnesses extended and welcomed. May we all have the discernment and courage to respond to the holy nudge, and humble and sensitive enough to accept and appreciate the kindnesses extended to us.

Kindness to Your Neighbor

"It is a sin to despise one's neighbor, but blessed is the one who is kind to the needy" (Prov 14:21). Jesus taught that we should love our enemies, bless those who curse us, do good to those who hate us, and pray for those who mistreat and persecute us (Matt 5:44; Luke 6:27–28). This is indeed a hard teaching. I have trouble enough loving my family, let alone my neighbors and my enemies, but there it is! Bless those who curse us and do good to those who hate us, and that, it seems to me, includes those who live next door with a barking dog, an unkempt lawn, and an RV parked out front, and those who are talking behind our backs and working to undermine our ministry at church—but how?

According to Proverbs 14:21, the key is to be kind to the needy, and that is all of us. We are all broken pots, all needy, so if this proverb has anything to say to us, it is that the proper spiritual weapon of choice is not spite, as tempting as such a stance may seem to be at the time, but kindness. And we are blessed when we act with kindness—consecrated and made holy. That's the key. Kindness extended to our neighbors may not change the way they act, make their RV disappear, or cause them to cease their malicious gossip in church, but it will change us. I believe that's why this proverb calls it a sin to despise our neighbors. It will not help the neighbor, and it will ultimately deform us. At the end of the day, we are shaped and formed by what we do—for good or for ill. Our attitudes and actions take us somewhere. They are never neutral; they are choices we make, and we are blessed when we choose kindness.

Honoring God

"Whoever oppresses the poor shows contempt for their Maker, but whoever is kind to the needy honors God" (Prov 14:31). One cannot read Scripture without coming away with the notion that God has a special heart for the poor and oppressed; the oppressors, not so much. As we will see in the next section, it matters to God how the poor are treated. God takes it personally.

I believe that all acts of kindness humbly offered honor God, but how so? How do we honor the God of the universe? Most of us are familiar with the fifth commandment, "Honor your father and your mother" (Exod 20:12a). For some reason, it has always been easy for me to find ways to honor my mother—a personal note, an unexpected phone call, a small bouquet of flowers, almost any type of little gift from a recent trip (which she always exhibited on the mantle for all to see), a walk in her garden or a nearby park, or a drive in the county. I guess I honored my mother by paying attention to the little things in her life, listening to her reflections about family and church, and by being present. That's all it took.

On the other hand, it was more difficult for me to find ways to honor my father. He wasn't much into small talk, or deep conversations for that matter, and he wasn't much for walks or personal notes either. He was a doer, loving to work with his hands. I struggled for a good part of my adult life trying to figure out how to honor him. I couldn't build anything. Finally, I realized that he was very proud of his sons, all his sons, including me. He watched from a distance, but he followed our comings and goings with deep interest and great care. In so many ways, he walked with each of us. It came to me that the best way to honor him was to simply live the kind of life that would affirm him and reflect his character. At the end of the day, I honored my father by being like him, living the kind of life that he would live.

I think there is a parallel here when we think about honoring God. We do so when we live our lives in ways that reflect and display the character of our loving God, and kindness is the key, the very heart of God, grace with hands and feet. When we love our neighbors and extend kindness to the poor and oppressed (which is all of us in some way or another), I'm sure it brings a smile to the face of our maker, who watches closely as we strive to live honorable and holy lives.

Lending to the Lord

"Whoever is kind to the poor lends to the Lord, and he will reward them for what they have done" (Prov 19:17). At first blush, this is a verse that I would like to put back in the bread loaf. How in the world can needy souls like us lend anything to the Lord? Isn't God the one with all the resources? What do we have that God would ever want? Good questions all.

On one level, it is helpful to think of the act of lending (sharing) as a way of investing, contributing, joining, and extending the work, hopes, and dreams of another. For example, when we "lend" some money to a granddaughter so she can participate in a regional youth conference, we do not do so with the hope of accruing some interest income. Rather, it is an avenue to honor and shepherd her desire for spiritual formation and social growth. The payoffs are eternal.

On another level, we "lend to the Lord" when we lend a hand and lean into the work that is before us. I remember several occasions when my father would come into the house and ask, "Hey, can someone lend me a hand?" In other words, I need your help—now! And, of course, we would all race out and do what we could. I sometimes wonder if God isn't saying much the same thing, "Hey, I need your help. If you want to lend a hand, please feed the hungry, nourish the thirsty, welcome the stranger, clothe the naked, care for the sick, and visit those in prisons of one kind or another." And as Jesus told his disciples in the parable of the Sheep and the Goats, "Truly I tell you, whatever you did for one of the least of these brothers and sisters of mine, you did for me" (Matt 25:35–39).

There are always spiritual implications when we offer kindness and lend a hand—doing what we can. Kindness, as it turns out, is sacred. And this is particularly important when the church is in a mess. When gossip, anger, and hurt feelings swirl, the temptation is to join in the fray and even go on the offensive in an attempt to protect ourselves. Sadly, this only stirs things up even more. The antidote is patience and kindness—offering grace, hoping for the best, and loving all the wounded souls present. After all, we are, all of us, hungry, thirsty, strangers, naked, sick, or in bondage of one kind or another. I don't believe that God calls us to avenge every wrong and clean up every mess. Church life can be a circus at times, but we are not called to save it. Rather, with patience and kindness we are to lean in and lend a hand, displaying the character of the God who would not let our sin stand in the way of a relationship with him.

Some Next Steps

Before we conclude this chapter on kindness with some questions for reflection and discussion (a good way to engage your close friends or small group), let me offer several Next Steps or ways to put the daily practice of kindness into practice. As you will see, these steps are not rocket science, but they do offer some tangible ways to transition from merely thinking about kindness to choosing the be a kinder person each day—starting today.

Focus on Your Own Life

I don't know about you, but when I hear a powerful sermon that challenges the way we who claim Christ are supposed to live, I immediately think of others who could benefit from the message. In fact, I often find myself saying, "I sure hope ____ (you put in the name) was listening today!" I guess it is human nature to focus on the shortcomings of others rather than on our own, pointing out a speck of sawdust in their eye rather than the plank in our own (Matt 7:3). When we start to be intentional about choosing kindness, the same malady can surface. It is easy to see all the ways that others could be kinder, and sometimes we even point it out to anyone who will listen. This is not the way to start. Focus on your own life.

And I suggest that you don't share your new project with anyone (unless you feel that you are in need of an accountability partner) or make a public spectacle of your acts of kindness. Just start each day with intention, choosing to be kinder, and let the Holy Spirit do the heavy lifting. Just because we focus on our own lives, it doesn't mean that we need to seek the spotlight or anyone's approval. That would be a serious mistake, and I fear that our good intentions can be hampered by such self-aggrandizing behaviors. Keep the focus on you, but not about you.

Start Small

You don't have to change the entire world on day one, or on any day for that matter. Our calling is to be a faithful presence where we live, right in our own neighborhoods. We are not called to save the circus. When Jesus told his disciples that he was the vine and they were the branches (John 15:5a), that was good news for all of us. He is a vine that sustains all the branches. Our job is to stay connected to the vine and love God and neighbor with everything we have.

As with any disciplined practice, the best advice is to start small, right where you live. One might decide on the goal of running a marathon someday, but it won't be the first day. Any effort such as this requires a series of disciplined steps in training that help build the necessary stamina, strength, and resolve to finish the race. So it is with the decision to be kind. It won't happen all at once, but it will happen. Just start with small steps in your own neighborhood, and let the Holy Spirit take the lead. It will be a spiritual venture of a lifetime, even if you don't leave your own front porch. God honors small steps.

Be Kind to Yourself

When you choose to be kinder to others, don't forget to be kinder to yourself, too. Sometimes we're our own worst critic. It is easy to get frustrated when you see little progress, or you slip up. You don't have to go back to the starting line and start over. Be patient. We are not called to be perfect; we are called to be faithful. Just keep leaning in with intention and look and listen for God's guidance and assurance. Remember—choosing daily to be kinder is a practice that will become a way of life. Give it time. Just be faithful.

Make Kindness Your Passion

I recently attended an event where all the staff wore badges that had a line for their name, a line for their title, and a line for their passion. Each worker's passion was different, of course—storytelling, family, baseball, reading, church, hiking, etc. It made for a great conversation starter, and it told everyone a little bit about that person and what was important to them. I wonder what would happen if we made kindness our passion. I don't think we need to wear a badge proclaiming it. That seems like a bit too much self-promotion, but I do believe that our passions shape and form us for good and for ill. Make kindness your passion and don't be afraid to share with others when the time is right. Such an approach to life may be simple, but it is powerful and sacred because kindness extended reveals the very character of God.

Conclusion

According to the Apostle Paul, love at its best requires both patience and kindness. They are like two sides of the same coin. Patience extends the opportunity to practice kindness in any one place, and kindness gives patience direction, power, and purpose. Certainly, a church in a mess desperately needs both. Being kind cannot be faked, at least not for very long, and I don't believe that we can just decide one day to be kind. Rather, we choose each day to be kinder, and the intentional practice of kindness over time reproduces itself in sacred ways.

Acts of kindness are never wasted, and a single act has the power to change the trajectory of someone's life, even our own. And kindness has a long shelf life. It's unpredictable—you never know when or where or how an act of kindness will manifest or replicate itself, but it has power because it is real, summoned from within. It reveals and honors the character of God and shapes and forms us when we are intentional about its practice. Kindness is a sacred act because we are all connected in some deep way, and I have come to believe that the Holy Spirit dwells in and works through acts of kindness.

At the end of the day and at the end of our days, if someone were to summarize our lives by saying that we were kind, nothing more would need to be said. And this holds particularly true if someone were to say that about our behavior while attending a church in a mess. That would say it all. After all, love at its best is kind.

Questions for Reflection and Discussion:

1. Can you recall a time when a simple act of kindness changed a situation, or changed you?
2. Why is it so difficult to be kind in the midst of a messy church?
3. If you were to choose to be kinder today, does a particular relationship or situation come to mind where kindness is needed rather than seeking vengeance or justice? What would be your first step?
4. How could you be a source of encouragement for someone today? Remember—it costs nothing but means everything.
5. We were encouraged in this chapter to be kind to ourselves, too. What aspect of your spiritual life do you tend to be your own worst critic? How about a kindness break today? What would being kind to yourself look like for you?

Love is patient, love is kind . . .

PART II

Love Out of Bounds

The church in Corinth was in a mess; it was a mess. Competition, jealousy, misguided theologies, and disputatious personalities ruled the day. The church wrote to Paul and asked for his advice, and Paul wasn't shy about giving it. He responded that signs and wonders, prophecies, visions, and personal displays of spirituality and leadership were all well and good in their place—as long as love was at the center. But without love, Paul contended in so many words, all you have is a big mess.

According to Paul, patience and kindness are the very heart and soul of love. These practices, when taken seriously and consistently, provide the balm for healing and the hope and promise of better days ahead. Without them, however, our actions are empty, gaining nothing (1 Cor 13:3b). And Paul continued by offering some insight into the kind of love that was necessary to withstand the havoc of a messy church. Love not only needed both heart and soul, it also needed clear boundaries—certain attitudes and behaviors such as envy, boasting, pride, disrespect, self-seeking, temper tantrums, revenge, and delight in evil were simply out of bounds. Without a corporate sense of what is out of bounds, a church in a mess can easily find itself straying into swampy territory and getting stuck in the mud or entering into a spiritual mud fight of one kind or another.

We will examine eight of these out-of-bounds actions and attitudes in Part II, Love Out of Bounds, beginning with envy, one of the seven deadly sins. Without doubt, envy is dangerous when it rears its ugly head in any body of believers, but when a church is in a mess, it can prove to be as deadly as the plague. Perhaps that is why Paul began his list of out-of-bounds behaviors and attitudes with this nasty fellow.

— 3 —

Love Does Not Envy

The spirit of envy can destroy; it can never build.

—Margaret Thatcher

Introduction

I GREW UP IN a small farming community in central Michigan in the 1950s. I was a boomer, and even though I was not born until after World War II, it was always a subject of conversation, even for the kids on my block. Whenever we played "army and navy," our adversaries were German, Italian, and Japanese.

And my folks and all our neighbors lived through the Great Depression, too, so even though my dad had a steady job, a good job, there was always an unspoken fret that things could go sour at any time. As I think back, there were kids everywhere all the time—between twelve to eighteen on our block alone, depending on the year. We never lacked for things to do or partners in fun or crime, such as our crimes were. All the families on our block were as poor as church mice, so there wasn't much need or call for envy since we were all in the same boat, living paycheck to paycheck. All that changed, however, when I went to school, especially around the fourth grade.

One of the boys in my class, let's call him Danny, just didn't fit in with the rest of us. He wasn't very athletic, so he rarely joined in with our games at recess, and my brother and I regularly cleaned him out of his entire leather sack of cat's eye marbles, and won his new leather sack, too. It was done without cheating; he was just that terrible at marbles. One day, his mother drove over to our house and demanded that we stop stealing Danny's marbles. My mother stood up for us and told Danny's mother that the transactions were on the up-and-up. If he couldn't afford to lose, he shouldn't play marbles with the Allen boys after school. After all, we were the best shooters on the entire south side of town. Nonetheless, she made us give back all his marbles and surrender three leather marble sacks, and instructed us under threat of corporal punishment to never play marbles with Danny again. We took her threat seriously and turned our attention elsewhere.

There's another reason why Danny didn't quite fit in. His parents ran a very successful business in town, one of the few entrepreneurial efforts that could be described as such. As a result, his parents had money. He regularly wore new clothes to school, complete with new jackets and boots for every season. We wore pants with knee patches and rips long before it was fashionable to do so. He had a very expensive lunch box that put our paper lunch bags to shame, and he had a way of flaunting his store-bought bread sandwiches, bottles of pop, and candy bars at lunch. We all rode our secondhand bikes to school, and on the days when his mother didn't drive him to school in their new convertible, he rode a brand new bike decked out with handlebar streamers, saddlebags, a headlight, and big red reflectors—and an expensive bike lock that he used to secure his bike to the tree by the front door of the school. He said that he didn't want to leave his bike parked next to any of ours. I believe that that was the first time that I was envious of anyone or anything. I don't know what bothered me more; the fact that he had so many nice things to flaunt, or the fact that I didn't and couldn't.

One spring day, Danny couldn't find his new jacket after school, even after a thorough search of the long row of hooks where we hung our coats and lined up our boots, the cupboards at the back of the room, and the supply closet. The jacket was nowhere to be found. Danny finally just tilted his head and told everyone that he would buy another one that afternoon. He ran out the front door and climbed into his mother's waiting car, giving a big wave as they drove off. Apparently, it was no big deal.

But it turned out to be a big deal to me. I suppose it was a big deal because if I lost a jacket or a pair of boots or couldn't find my ball glove, I would simply go without. There were no replacements to be had—we couldn't buy a new one. As I heard many times growing up, *Money doesn't grow on trees.* And I suppose it turned out to be big deal because of what happened next. As I was cutting across the playground on my way home, I saw Danny's jacket wadded up on the ground next to the fence—right where he had left it when the sun came out in the middle of a game of tag. I walked over to the fence and picked up the jacket. It was so new that it was stiff, something that I hadn't experienced since almost all my clothes were hand-me-downs from my older brother. My clothes were always clean and mended, but they were not new. In fact, the only "new" shirt I received each year was the shirt my mother made for my school picture. After that, I only wore the shirt to church.

To this day, I honestly don't believe what happened next. I took the jacket and tossed it in some mud. Then I stomped on the jacket, threw it over the fence, and walked away. I don't know if Danny ever got the coat back or if he even cared, but I have carried the memory of that deed my entire adult life. Why did I do that? As my mother would ask me from time to time, "What got into you?" This would have been one of those occasions, but I never told anyone. What got into me? Honestly, I don't really know, but I think that envy had a lot to do with it. As we will see in the following section, envy can be a destructive emotion that stems from desiring what others have *or* wishing that others lacked it. I think the latter describes my situation. When it came right down to it, I didn't like Danny. Part of it, of course, was his bragging, but if I am honest, there was envy at work, too, although I'm not sure I even knew how to describe it at the time.

Looking back, envy produced discontent, discontent gave way to resentment, and resentment led to unkindness. Certainly, my behavior was way out of bounds, over the line. As it turns out, it is difficult to *like* someone you envy, and impossible to *love* someone you envy. Envy simply takes you the wrong way down a bad road. Perhaps that's why the Apostle Paul was so adamant that love does not envy. I think it is equally true that envy does not love, and a church in a mess needs love more than anything.

An Emotion Named Envy

Aristotle described envy as feelings of pain at the good fortune of others. It can certainly be a painful experience for carriers of such an emotion in ways known and unknown, and it is painful for those around them, too. Envy, as it turns out, is rarely a general or vague feeling. It is typically aimed at someone, something, or some circumstance. And as it runs its course, envy gets personal.

Envy is a feeling, an emotion, a longing stemming from the belief that someone else has more, has done more, is better, or is just plain luckier than you. It is a deficit emotion, a painful awareness that others are superior in one way or another, and you either desire what they have or wish that they didn't have it or somehow could lose it—and you don't mind helping out if the opportunity arises. The first two early warning signs that envy is at work are discontent and resentment. Of course, we can be discontented for many reasons, and not all discontentment is bad. In fact, sometimes feelings of discontent are a reminder of the end of a season of life or a signal that it is time to refocus or move on. Discontent of this kind is actually a gift, providing an itch and an inclination to change or get going again. However, if our discontent stems from a deeply held and deeply felt conviction that we always get the short end of the stick and life is patently unfair, resentment is just around the corner. As it turns out, the mixture of discontent and resentment is a wicked cocktail, leading to a host of helpless and hopeless responses in our work, in our families, and in our spiritual lives. Resentment and discontent stemming from envy simply robs us of the ability to accept what is, see a new horizon, and move on, three of the healthiest spiritual disciplines I know.

To be honest, it is not always easy to rejoice at the good fortune of others since envy is deeply rooted in the human condition. It is quite human to ask, "Why them? Why now? Why not me?" Yet the Apostle Paul is quite clear—love does not envy, so how do we keep envy from driving our love for each other out of bounds, especially in a messy church situation? As we will see in the next section, there are social and spiritual forces at work that are not helpful, but the situation is far from hopeless.

Love Out of Bounds

At first blush, it may seem that feelings of envy are not all that dangerous or hurtful. After all, it doesn't hurt anyone to wish for another's fortune, looks, abilities, etc. Or does it? As it turns out, small pains of envy are warning signs that something is seriously wrong. And like heart disease, there is a huge price to be paid if the warning signs are ignored. The first indicator is pettiness. We start by picking at and grumbling about others, minimizing and marginalizing what they have done—or what they are trying to do. This discontent leads to resentment, and resentment opens the door to a nasty jealousy that ushers in an entire portfolio of unkindness including criticism, gossip, backstabbing, undermining, and marginalization. Envy may begin as a passive dislike, but an active hatred can germinate that is devastating for any church in a mess. The link is jealousy. Jealousy brings no understanding, fosters no sympathy, and cultivates neither healing nor hope. And while the old English saying is true—envy shoots at others and wounds itself—unfortunately the envier is not the only casualty. Others get hurt, too. Envy is out of bounds.

Sadly, I am afraid that our obsession with social media invites and fosters envy. We are smiling in every picture we post, and we post dozens and dozens of pictures displaying our latest activities, travels, and accomplishments. Every single picture is a happy pose. It is like Disneyland, and no more representative of reality. However, it is so easy to accept all these posts as reality, so when we compare our lives with what we see reported each day, we conclude that the entire world is having a wonderful time doing magnificent things and we are as boring as hell. When we start counting others' blessings and forgetting our own, we are in serious trouble. There is no joy in comparing our reality to our friends' Facebook posts. When we do, envy is lurking just around the corner.

And this type of unfair and unnecessary comparison can happen in our churches, too. Messy times seem to foster an unspoken, unhealthy spiritual competition, each person working to be sure that others know just how spiritual they are. Everyone wears a mask with a big smile, yet all the while there is turmoil just beneath the surface. I call it "the holier than thou contest" and sadly there are no winners. Everybody loses. It was going on in the church in Corinth in Paul's time, and it continues to this very day—and a church in a mess seems especially fertile soil for envy and all its cousins. Simply put, an unhealthy church seems to invite and support superficial relationships, unhealthy spiritual behaviors, and corrosive theologies. It is a mess that fosters more messes.

So, if envy is deeply rooted in the human condition and fostered by our social and spiritual environments, can there be any hope? Is envy simply an incurable disease? Must it necessarily lead to resentment, jealousy, and meanness of one kind or another? Thankfully, I think there is a way forward. Paul was confident that love is the key to the messes we face, and love does not envy. I think he's right.

What Can We Do About Envy?

For those of us who struggle with feelings of envy at one time or another, and that is most of us, there are at least four strategies that we can undertake to keep envy from its destructive path. First, understand it—see envy for what it is and for what it isn't. It is not uncommon for flashes of envy to come, especially when hearing about someone's good fortune, but you don't have to believe everything that you feel. In other words, don't be shocked when you sense some feelings of envy, just don't carry them or let them carry you. Feelings come and feelings go; understand them for what they are and don't let them color your vision of the world or of yourself.

Second, name envy when you feel it. My mother was fond of the old saying that confession is good for the soul. It is. There should be no embarrassment about admitting when you feel a twinge of envy. In fact, it is the best thing to do. Get it out in the open. Honesty is the best policy—another of mother's favorite sayings. I know it is hard to share your less than perfect moments with someone you love and trust, but let's face it—we are not perfect. The good news is that we are not called to be perfect, but to be faithful, mature, tender, and kind. Sharing when you first come up short is a good way of preventing a long journey down a very bad road.

Third, get out of the comparison business. It's a game you can never win because there will always be someone who are smarter, more successful, richer, funnier, and wiser—always. One of the most healing and comforting approaches to life is to be grateful for what you have instead of focusing on what you don't have. In the end, it is not about having, but about caring and kindness. Find a place to volunteer, serve, and help others in need. It's always a good wake-up call and corrective for feelings of envy.

At the end of the day, I believe that healing comes with the pursuit of holiness. Now I know that this is a loaded word, but I remain convinced that we are called to be holy as God is holy (1 Pet 1:16). I readily admit that God is better at this than we are. After all, it is God's nature to be holy. For us, it's a lifelong journey to be conformed to the image of Christ. But there are spiritual practices (some we will share as Next Steps later in this chapter) that can mitigate feelings of envy and other self-defeating behaviors, and shape us in godly ways. A good place to start is to meditate seriously and consistently on Micah 6:8, asking God to show you what it means to pursue justice, mercy, and humility every day—to make them the centerpiece of your life. You will be amazed at the possibilities for service and ministry that present themselves each day. Such a practice leaves little room for envy, and I am convinced that slowly, steadily, and surely, we can become holier than we now are rather than merely trying to appear holier than everyone else—and envying them when we don't pull it off. Love does not envy because envy is out of bounds.

Scripture

I want us to examine the Old Testament story of Joseph and the actions of his brothers. There is no doubt that envy, jealousy, hatred, even thoughts of murder, were at work, leading to events imagined and unimagined. Did the brothers have any choices or were they the victims of poor decisions and inappropriate behavior? We shall see.

Joseph and His Ornate Robe

If you ever attended church as a child for even a short while, then you've probably heard the story of Joseph and his ornate robe, generally referred to in Sunday school and Vacation Bible School as his coat of many colors. It was given to him by his father, Jacob, because he loved Joseph more than any of his other sons, reportedly because he came to this earth late in his father's life. Certainly, we can say that he was his father's pride and joy.

To be candid, it isn't entirely clear whether it was a coat of many colors, or an otherwise ornate robe, or simply a robe with long sleeves. What is clear, however, is that it was a sign of special favor, and his brothers didn't like it a bit. There were even rumors that Joseph would someday assume the mantle of family leadership and inherit all their father's land, cattle, property, and other possessions. You can see why this wouldn't sit well with his brothers, all of whom were older and ahead of him in the line of succession. And it didn't help that Joseph was a tattletale and wore his ornate robe everywhere, even when he was out on a reconnaissance trip for his father, far from home, or that he shared his two dreams that the entire family, including the sun and moon, would bow down and worship him. Joseph could have saved himself a good deal of grief if he had simply left his robe in his tent and kept his dreams to himself, but that is a speculation for another day. The facts are that he didn't, and he ended up in a deep cistern, then sold into slavery to a passing caravan. His brothers' actions were the result of the progression from envy to jealously to hatred. As always, it was a bad sequence of emotions that spelled trouble (Gen 37). They were out of bounds.

Honestly, I empathize with Joseph's brothers. It wasn't fair, but there it was. It is easy to understand their feelings of envy, but how did they deal with those feelings? They could have silently accepted the favored treatment as the prerogative of their father, as hard as that would have been to swallow, then packed up their belongings and set out on their own. They could have protested to their father, trying to communicate how hurtful his actions were, and requested a clear understanding about the lines of succession. Or they could have confronted Joseph about his obvious flaunting, hoping that he would recognize how hurtful and aggravating his behavior was to the entire family. So even in a difficult, uncertain, and irritating circumstance, they had options, but envy whispered that they were out of luck, leading to jealousy, then hatred—and that is how they justified their mean, deceitful, even terrible behavior.

I don't think I need to connect all the dots as to how this story relates to a church in a mess. Suffice it here to say that things aren't always fair in church. In fact, they rarely are, but that doesn't mean that we have no options other than to even the score. There are always options, not Disneyland options, but options, nonetheless. However, if we let envy run its course, love ends up out of bounds and many get hurt.

Next Steps

The next steps that follow are not all that profound. Next steps usually aren't, but if taken seriously and practiced daily, they will shape and form us in good ways. The things we practice take us somewhere. Perhaps some other next steps come to mind for you, too. That is fine. The key, I have come to believe, is that we must be involved in our own spiritual formation, not merely spectators, reacting to whatever happens to us. Even though we can't control everything that happens, we are not helpless either. Here are three things all of us can do if we are concerned about curbing feelings of envy in our lives.

Put Your Phone Down

Start with a one-week social media fast. That's right, an entire week without reading or posting anything! It will be hard at first, I admit, but if you are serious about limiting the envy-producing power of social media in your life, just don't read or post. Get off social media and leave it alone. You will find that you can survive without seeing every post from vacations, work trips, and family functions from all your friends, or sharing the latest cute picture of your cat and then checking hourly to see how many likes you've received.

After a week of going social media cold turkey, then go slow turkey. That is, limit your social media viewing to fifteen minutes a day. Set aside a quarter of an hour to quickly skim social media, respond to a particularly important post or offer one, and then put your phone down again. Don't let it become a crutch to pass away the time, and if you want to know what the temperature is outside, step outside for a moment rather than looking it up on a weather app. Remember that the aim of social media is to pull you in until you wear out your thumbs, and such obsessive behavior can be an invitation to a host of unhealthy emotions—loneliness, disillusion, and envy, to name just a few. My father would say that if you wanted to lose some weight, it is better to avoid the donut shop. I say that if you deal with feelings of envy, avoid social media altogether or manage it carefully. Social media is not your friend.

Maintain a Gratitude List

Make a list of the things for which you are thankful, and review and update it regularly. Carry the list with you, keeping it in your notebook or pocket. And at least once a day, every day, take out the list and consider it carefully and prayerfully, thanking God for the blessings in your life. As it turns out, counting your blessings is one of the best correctives for envy there is.

Show up and Pitch In

Find a place to serve underprivileged and needy families. The opportunities, even in a small community, perhaps especially in a small community, are virtually endless. Check with a pastor at your church, with another church, or with a social service agency serving your town or county. And if you have a special gift or interest, think about how you could use it to serve others. It is always gratifying to help others in need, and it is a good way to reflect on our own blessings. And you will find that when you intentionally set out to give to others, you end up on the receiving end, too. Grace works that way.

Conclusion

Love does not envy, and as it turns out, envy does not love. In fact, envy—a deficit emotion, the painful awareness that others are superior in one way or another and you either desire what they have or wish that they didn't have it or somehow could lose it—can lead to the two terrible twins: discontent and resentment. And the twins can foster a jealousy that brings with it a portfolio of unkindness, driving love out of bounds.

Since envy visits most of us at one time or another, the key is to see it clearly for what it is and what it isn't, call it out when you experience it, get out of the comparison business (getting off social media will help avoid thinking that all your friends are living in Disneyland and you're in the dumps), and focus your efforts on pursuing holiness one day at a time. A good place to start is by making justice, forgiveness, and humility primary spiritual goals (Mic 6:8).

At the end of the day, we are called to love God and neighbor with everything we have (Mark 12: 30–31). Sadly, envy is a spiritual impediment to the kind of persons we are called to become. Fortunately for all of us, there are good ways that we can participate in our own spiritual formation rather than just reacting to what comes our way. Surely, envy will make a visit at one time or another, but we need not let it take root and drive love out of bounds. Even in a messy church situation, perhaps especially in a messy church situation, we need to hear clearly and take the Apostle Paul's admonition seriously, "Love does not envy." Neither should we, and the good news is that we don't have to. Thanks be to God.

Questions for Reflection and Discussion:

1. Are you more prone to envy other's abilities, possessions, or just plain dumb luck?
2. If you were to make a gratitude list, what would be your top five items?
3. If you were to fast from social media for a week, what would be your biggest challenge while doing so?
4. If you currently serve, what do you most gain from the experience, and if you don't, where might you find a place of service to those less fortunate or in need? How can you make it a priority to do so?
5. How might you become more of an actor and less a spectator in your own spiritual formation? What are some next steps for you? Write them down and review them often.

Love is patient, love is kind. It does not envy . . .

— 4 —

Love Does Not Boast

*Much of someone's real character lies in what
they don't say about themselves.*

—Joyce Rachelle

Introduction

In 1 Corinthians 13, the Apostle Paul includes envy, pride, and boasting in the same sentence, and with good reason, firmly asserting that these nasty weeds crowd out love and replace it with actions and attitudes that are totally out of bounds. And in a church in a mess, they grow like topsy. Envy and pride are feelings that take you to a bad place; boasting is an action that indicates that you are already in a bad place—even if you don't realize it, and it is hard on others, too. In many ways, boasting is like walking around with a rip in your pants or a price tag hanging from the underarm of your new blazer. You don't see it, but almost everyone else does, and they wonder if they should mention it to you, and if so, just how to do so without hurting your feelings. As it turns out, receiving that kind of news may be awkward, but such loving acts are also the best way to avoid further humiliation. We all need truth-telling friends in our lives.

In this chapter, we'll try to gain some understanding about why boasting is so common in our culture, including our churches, what compels and supports this boasting culture, and what can we do as Christians to deal with boasting in our own lives. As we will see, boasting is a difficult habit to break, requiring insight, humility, and maturity. Fortunately, there are spiritual practices that move us away from such self-inflicting behaviors like boasting and toward actions and reflections that shape us in the likeness of Christ. And as you might suspect, love is the key—and love does not boast.

A Confession

There is a fine line between being a good storyteller on the one hand and boasting on the other. Sometimes, the line totally disappears. I have always been a storyteller of sorts. My brother reminded me that we once dug a big hole in the back yard behind the raspberry bushes, and I would charge the neighborhood kids a nickel to climb into the hole and hear one of my stories. When times were tough, I would only charge a penny, and when times were really tough, I would give back all the coins and start the process all over again. I guess I enjoyed the audience more than the financial rewards.

Sometimes I got a bit carried away in my storytelling. On one occasion, a neighbor (let's call him Howard) on the next street over had a deer hanging from a tree in his backyard. It was a way of curing the meat—and letting everyone know that the hunt was successful. I stood admiring the deer when Howard walked over and asked, "What do you think?" "It's a nice one," I replied, "but my dad just shot a bear and it's hanging in our garage!" I didn't anticipate what a stir shooting a bear would cause. After several failed drive-by attempts to catch a glimpse of the bear, Howard came to the door and asked if he could see the bear. Of course, there was no bear, and I was caught telling a whopper, a big boast. Actually, it was a lie.

On another occasion, imagine how surprised my mother and father were when they visited my third-grade classroom for Parents Night and saw this poster hanging from the ceiling: Patrick saw a bat fly across his living room one evening last week (and it wasn't a baseball bat!). Another lie in the form of a boast. Why? Why would a young child, or anyone else for that matter, tell a whopper, a deception, an embellished story, a little lie? I believe that such behaviors stem from some deep feelings of inferiority and insecurity, and signal an unmet desire for attention, to be in the limelight, singled out as special. To be honest, I've struggled with that temptation all my life.

In some ways, these desires motivated me to be a good student, a better athlete, and a solid professional in my work. And over time, the necessity to make things up to make me look better to others and feel better about myself has subsided, but I must admit that as I think and talk about my basketball playing years now long gone, I get better with each passing year! I guess there's still some work to do.

There are two kinds of boasting, however, that don't cross the line of truth, but they are just as damaging, perhaps more so. I'm talking about incessant self-promotion and relentless one-upmanship, and I've been tempted by both. When someone you know continually promotes themselves, the temptation is to do the same. It is a powerful temptation. When someone brags about their book, I am tempted to brag about mine. And when someone boasts about the nationally known authors and musicians they know, I am tempted to join in and name-drop, too. When they talk about their travels to China, I am tempted to talk about my trip to Angkor Wat. The temptations are real, but the ultimate toll is substantial, while the rewards are, at best, fleeting. Ultimately, there are no winners in the boasting game. Everyone is diminished.

I heard Dallas Willard tell about a time when he was in seminary. Every Monday morning, the students would return to class and brag about where they preached on Sunday, how many people attended, and how much they were paid. The game was to jockey all week to receive a "good" invitation, and then come back to do a little holy bragging. He admitted that he was tempted to join in the contest when he received an admonition from the Lord. Looking back, he said that he knew it was from the Lord because he wasn't mature enough at that age to come up with it all by himself. This is what came to him: *Don't try to promote yourself or pursue any speaking engagements. Just be sure to have something to say if you are ever asked.* And as we know, he was asked to speak all over the world, and he always had something to say.

One final confession. During the last five years of my professional career, I moved from a high-level administrative position at the university to join the EdD faculty in the College of Education. For anyone with a clear perspective, it was a wonderful move, having much more relational and writing time, and much less stress. However, since I left my administrative post with a bit of a nudge, my new position brought up once again some old feelings of embarrassment and inadequacy. When I was introduced to someone as a professor in the EdD program, I would quickly add that I was once the provost or that I had written some books. As you can plainly see, it was very sad, and it took me a year or two to realize just how blessed I was and how fortunate it was to work with such gifted students and dedicated colleagues. My boasting was totally unnecessary, yet tempting—at age eight or sixty-eight. Humility is a hard-won virtue.

In this chapter, we will examine together various types of boasting, what drives these acts, and what damage it does to self, others, and the church. And as we will see, there are spiritual forms of boasting, too. No wonder Paul was quick to write, *Love does not boast*, because as Paul knew, such boasting is simply out of bounds. It spoils the sweet milk of fellowship, and in a messy church situation, it is so easy, so tempting, to join the vinegar crowd no matter how old you are or what you have accomplished. Fortunately, while boasting can bring out the worst in us, there are spiritual practices that give insight, courage, and confidence to us as we journey through the mess. God help us all.

Boasting

Boasting isn't just talk—it's big talk. It is typically defined as excessive pride and self-satisfied talk about achievements, possessions, or abilities. Please note the word *excessive*. There is nothing wrong with expressing a certain sense of pride in your own work or describing a feeling of self-satisfaction for what your kids have accomplished, but when it is excessive, it is out of bounds, at best mind-numbing. Just look at the synonyms for boasting: arrogant, conceited, cocky, immodest, and showing off, to mention only a few. It's not a positive list. And the synonyms for mind-numbing are just as painful: boring, dreary, drudging, dry, dull, jading, monotonous, ponderous, stuffy, tedious, tiring, uninteresting, and wearisome. I think you get the picture. A little prideful talk, like chili pepper, goes a long way; too much spoils the dish.

Boasting comes in all shapes and sizes. We can boast about what we have, what we've done, where we live, what we're doing, what we're going to do, what we know, and who we know. At its heart, boasting represents an inflated version or vision of our own lives, and it reveals a fundamental lack of self-confidence and humility. When we lose a trustworthy sense of who we are and what is important in life, we lose our way. We strike out in all directions, rationalize the consequences, and end up boasting about them. Truly, it is painful to witness.

And if we use any type of social media, witness we must. I admit that there is a fine line between reporting on your trip and simply boasting. Personally, if you have to post more than three or four pictures to capture the sentiments of your day, you might be nearing the line. If you post more than ten, you are over the line, and I don't even know what to say about posts containing twenty or thirty or forty or more smiling pictures. My advice: unfollow these friends until they return home and assume some type of normal life. It is wonderful to take a trip to the lake or to Europe, but please don't boast about it. It is mind-numbing for all of us who are left behind. Not even your mother wants to see forty photos of your two-hour visit to the Coliseum in Rome. One or two will do just fine.

Boasting is the kind of behavior that is in some odd way satisfying, but the residual impact is damaging. I can think of university colleagues who constantly and shamelessly promoted themselves and all their publications, invitations, and activities. To say that they had an inflated opinion of themselves would be a severe understatement. Yet, even though they felt good about themselves, they quickly became the butt of campus jokes. Their reputations suffered. They lost credibility and status, the very things that they were working so hard to warrant. Boasting is not a way to win friends and influence people, but it is a sure way to put a target on your back. And when we continually boast, we publicly reveal our own incompetence at discerning appropriate social behavior. We don't get it, but everyone else does.

Spiritual Boasting

I would like to tell you that boasting does not show its ugly head in the church community, but sadly it does—and it is not new. Jesus addressed spiritual boasting candidly and forcefully in his discourse now known as the Sermon on the Mount (Matt 5–7). He warned his followers to avoid grandstanding when gifts were offered to the needy (Matt 6:1–4), to refrain from excessive public prayers while standing on street corners (Matt 6:5–8), and to resist the temptation to make a public spectacle when engaging in spiritual practices such as fasting (Matt 6:16–18). According to Jesus, these spiritual acts are good, but if we make them about ourselves, they lose much of their formative power.

In particular, I want us to take note of three all-too-common forms of spiritual boasting that drive love out of bounds. First, there can be an unwelcome competition about who is most spiritual, having the most direct line of communication with God. As such, they are special, and they lord it over everyone with special words from God and filling their daily language with "spiritual speak—God talk." It can be a subtle form in boasting and intimidation. My advice when you encounter such behavior is to recognize it for what it is (spiritual boasting) and for what it isn't (God speaking through that person to everyone else). Of course, there are those who have walked with God for a very long time and have a good deal of wisdom and insight to offer, but if humility does not temper their desire to share all that God is telling them, beware. And as far as I know, there is no extra credit for drawing undue attention to ourselves during worship either. Honestly, I am overjoyed when the Spirit moves within a congregation, but more times than not, it is my experience that it turns out to be more about us than about the Spirit.

A second form of spiritual boasting has to do with who we know and what we know. It is so easy to flaunt the connections we have, the people we know—to name-drop, and to enter into long discourses about the history of the church, about the denomination, and about particular theological beliefs and assumptions. Imagine how someone who is new to the faith must feel when they encounter such behavior, often intended to engender spiritual hero worship. They are hoping to avoid embarrassment, desperately trying to figure out if the Gospel of Mark is in the New or Old Testament, and we come in and show off with all our knowledge. This behavior is out of bounds.

Finally, a third form of spiritual boasting has to do with self-promotion, telling anyone who will listen about how talented we are, how much we have done, and how much we could do if we were given half a chance to sing in the worship team, preach on Sunday morning, or lead the women's ministry efforts. No one self-promotes in an effort to be asked to set up chairs, clean up after an event, or bring the coffee. Honestly, many of us would like for others to recognize the gifts we have to offer, but excessive self-promotion is not the way forward. It drives love out of bounds.

It is easy to see why Paul wrote that love does not boast. Boasting, simply put, sours religious activities as individuals attempt to hijack the spotlight. And in a messy church situation, spiritual boasting seems to thrive. What can be done? Are there spiritual practices and strategies available to all of us when we find ourselves in a church mess and deeply desire to avoid spiritual grandstanding? The good news is that there are! After looking to a particular passage from Scripture for some wisdom and insight, I'll offer three spiritual practices that I believe will help all of us as we seek to keep love at the center of our congregational life and away from the thickets that line the boundaries.

Scripture

I want you to read these verses three times, out loud. This will be a familiar passage to most of us:

> "This, then, is how you should pray: 'Our Father in heaven, hallowed be your name, your kingdom come, your will be done, on earth as it is in heaven. Give us today our daily bread. And forgive us our debts, as we also have forgiven our debtors. And lead us not into temptation, but deliver us from the evil one.'" (Matt 6:9–13).

These words are the words of Jesus, and they are commonly referred to as the Lord's Prayer. They come to us as part of a larger discourse found in Matthew 5–7, the Sermon on the Mount. There are so many aspects of this prayer that are instructive, but I want us to focus our attention on just two: the placement of this prayer within the discourse and its embrace.

Interestingly, this instruction on how to pray immediately follows after Jesus warns all who would listen to avoid spiritual grandstanding when we pray, an obvious form of spiritual boasting. According to Jesus, there's no eternal reward for doing so (Matt 6:5). Instead, we are to affirm God's goodness and offer a simple, honest, humble request for daily bread, grace, and care. It is a prayer that comes from the heart; it's not a performance. There is no reason to turn such a prayer into a spectacle. That would be just plain wrong, way out of bounds.

The other aspect to consider is the embrace of the prayer. Look back and count how many times you see the words *I, me,* or *my* in the prayer. The answer is zero, none, not one. Instead we see *our, us, we,* and *your.* I don't think that the use of plural words is simply an accident of translation, some kind of oversight. I believe that Jesus was teaching all of us that the best way to avoid spiritual boasting when we pray is to include others, to pray for others as well as ourselves, to make it a corporate prayer. When the focus is on all of us instead of just me, it is difficult for boasting of any kind to take root. This is as it should be.

Next Steps

Sometimes I think church folk carry the idea that spiritual practices are some type of foreign, complicated spiritual activities that take place in secluded monasteries or in caves somewhere on the European coast, and they are reserved for the super spiritual or isolated religious kooks—or maybe both. As such, they have nothing to do with our day-to-day lives, and they are easily dismissed as unimportant or ineffective. However, nothing could be further from the truth. While it is true that spiritual practices are practiced by monks in distant monasteries all over the world, they are equally important for each of us, even if the biggest item on our daily agenda is to mow the lawn or take the kids for a haircut. All of life is sacred, all of it, and that includes all of our daily activities! Here are three spiritual practices or next steps for all of us who desire to deal with spiritual boasting, letting the Holy Spirit do the heavy lifting. I am convinced that if we do our part, God will be present and at work, too. You can count on it.

Cheer for Others

Everyone needs a cheerleader, so volunteer for the part, intentionally and purposely looking for opportunities to cheer for others. This is a form of encouragement which costs nothing but means everything. Try it. If you are prone to boasting (as I have been most of my life), you'll find it difficult to promote yourself while encouraging and cheering for others. It keeps the focus on them and the spotlight away from you. Admittedly, it isn't always easy and you may feel a twinge of envy if no one cheers for you in return, but if you are a faithful cheerleader, over time you will be shaped and formed in good and holy ways.

Ask Questions

Whenever you meet someone for lunch or coffee, it is tempting and far too easy to become the center of attention, dominating the conversation with stories past and present, some true and some mostly true. Of course, we all want to be liked, so entertaining others with your best stuff is really tempting. I've done it myself. However, it is simply a sad form of boasting.

Knowing my own proclivity to dominate a conversation, over the past several years I started to take time before a meeting or coffee date to come up with a list of at least five questions that I could ask to get the other person talking. Sometimes I even write out the questions so I won't forget them, and the list also serves as a gentle reminder that this time is not totally about me. And when we meet, I casually mention that I have some questions to ask. It is always met with a willing smile, and off we go. The best way I know to avoid the spotlight is to shine it on others.

Be Silent

Academics can be incessant self-promoters. The system actually encourages professors to self-promote, and they are not alone. As the old question goes, "If you don't toot your own horn, who will?" Over the years, I've decided that that's the wrong question to ask. A better question is this, "Can we let our life speak for itself?" I think we can, but it takes a good deal of maturity, dignity, and grace. Ironically, at the end of the day, what others will say about us will have very little to do with our resumes and everything to do with the kind of persons we were as we made our way in this world—things that are not found on our resumes. The most important things never are. We will be known by our fruits, reflected in how we treated others, so let your life speak for itself. No need to blow your own horn.

Honestly, these three next steps or spiritual practices are straightforward, but they are not easy. It is a difficult venture to refrain from boasting, especially in a messy church situation where it seems that everyone is about the business of spiritual self-promotion. There is no need to join these activities that drive love out of bounds. Instead, become a cheerleader for others, ask questions of others, and let your life speak for itself. This is a holy venture, and as you are guided by the Holy Spirit, you will grow in grace and be shaped in the image of Christ, who told anyone who would listen that giving, praying, and fasting are not for public consumption. Love does not boast.

Conclusion

Boasting is talk, big talk, excessive talk, aimed at self-promotion and one-upmanship, the art of gaining a feeling of superiority. Yet the end result, although rarely recognized, is that the boaster is diminished in the eyes of others, the very ones the boaster is so desperately and doggedly determined to impress. Somehow, boasting causes perceptual blindness.

Sadly, church communities are not immune from such behaviors, spiritual boasting in the form of self-promotion, holier-than-thou actions and language, and grandstanding—attempts to demonstrate that you know more people, theology, and everything else than anyone else. It kills the spirit, especially for those who are new to the faith, making them feel that they are somehow less-than and inadequate. While this is not always the intent, this *is* the result, and it seems that a church in a mess is the perfect environment for boasting—everyone for themselves. It is difficult to see how God is honored by such activities.

Fortunately, there are some next steps for those of us who want to be a positive force in a bad situation, to be shaped and formed by the Holy Spirit in the midst of chaos. These practices include becoming a cheerleader for others, intentionally turning the focus of conversations and meetings away from ourselves and toward others (a list of questions to ask in advance can be a helpful reminder and tool to let the light shine on others), and resolving to let your life speak for itself rather than telling everyone about all you have done and how spiritual you are. Over time—slowly, steadily, and surely, these next steps will challenge and change the heart of anyone who is inclined to boast, and that would be most of us, including me.

The Apostle Paul, writing centuries ago to a messy church in Corinth, was clear about the heart and soul of love—patience and kindness. He was equally direct about what drove love out of bounds and into the thickets. He began with envy and boasting for good reason. They spoiled the milk. They still do.

Questions for Reflection and Discussion:

1. What type of spiritual boaster irritates you the most: the I-am-holier-than-thou who flaunts a direct connection with God, the spiritual name-dropper, or the self-promoter?

2. Which type of spiritual boasting are you most prone to undertake? How can you guard against such behavior?

3. If you were to become a cheerleader this week, who would you cheer for and what three things could you do?

4. Imagine that you were to have lunch or coffee with someone soon. What questions could you list to keep the spotlight on them? If you don't have a meeting on your calendar, who could you invite?

5. We were encouraged to let our lives speak for themselves. What are three things your life would say about you?

Love is patient, love is kind. It does not envy,
it does not boast . . .

— 5 —

Love Is Not Proud

*Most of the trouble in the world is caused by
people wanting to be important.*

—T. S. Eliot

Introduction

My mother would often say that "pride goeth before a fall," a shortened version of Proverbs 16:18 (KJV). Of course, she was right to do so because pride, while not necessarily in and of itself bad, can easily become excessive, especially when the excess has to do with our own view of our abilities or our holiness. Pride is a subtle force but spiritually lethal, breeding overconfidence, conceit, and exaggerated feelings of superiority. Without doubt, these feelings drive love into the weeds and result in countless unnecessary spiritual blunders. Is it any wonder that pride is listed as one of the seven deadly sins and considered by many to be the one that is at the root of all the others?

In this chapter, we'll see why pride is such a great spiritual inhibitor, resisting honest and humble actions that invite grace into the messes of our lives. And we'll see that pride and humility are like oil and water—they don't mix. In fact, pride drives humility into the weeds.

Successful Pastors

I was having a coffee with a retired denominational leader at a local Newberg hangout, and I asked him what advice he would give to young pastors just starting out in the ministry. His answer was immediate: "I would tell them that the most important words they will ever speak are these—I'm sorry. I was wrong. Will you forgive me?" He went on to say that successful pastors learn and practice this early and often; others never get it.

He began to muse about his own pastoral journey. One day, the church office received an angry note from a couple who were long-standing members of the church. He immediately canceled his afternoon appointments, drove to their house, and knocked on the door. When they answered, their lips were pursed, and they looked like they were ready for a tense conversation. However, before they could say anything, he simply said, "I am so sorry. I apologize. Please forgive me." He said that it took them by surprise. They did forgive him, and they apologized, too. It seems there was more than enough blame to go around.

A year or so later, things were not going so well with the church, and the pastor was getting frustrated with all the complaining, criticism, and second guessing—all in Christian love, of course. That Friday, he looked at his calendar for the next week and saw that it was completely clear, something that had never happened before or since. He decided to take the week off for some solitude and prayer and told the congregation so that Sunday. The couple who wrote the angry letter came up immediately after the service and offered use of their lakeside cabin. It turned out to be a Godsend.

One evening, he was walking on the beach, throwing stones into the lake and throwing stones at his congregation, complaining to God about the situation. Suddenly, God spoke to him: "The problem is not the congregation; it's you. You have a bad attitude." It took him totally by surprise, but he took it nonetheless, and he thought and prayed about it for the rest of the week. On Sunday, he told the congregation about his conversation with God and said, "I am so sorry. I apologize. Please forgive me." What happened next was pure grace. Not only did the congregation embrace and forgive him, many confessed that it wasn't all his doing. They asked for forgiveness, too. As you might imagine, that was the start of a turnaround for the church and for his ministry among them.

Such moments take courage and humility, and grace abounds in them, but pride is often the great inhibitor. No wonder Paul writes "love is not proud"—because pride pushes love out of bounds.

The Neighbor's Motor Home

We live on a quiet street that is only one block long, with six houses, three on each side. As you might expect, we all see all the comings and goings, and we always greet each other with a wave and a smile. With a wave and a smile, that is, until our neighbor across the street (let's call him Frank), parked his gigantic motor home on the street directly across from the end of our driveway. I almost backed my pickup truck into it on more than one occasion, and it blocked our view of the neighborhood. At the very least, it was an eyesore, and as days turned into weeks, it proved to be a source of constant irritation. The city municipal code only allowed for parking on the street for up to seventy-two hours, and it was fast approaching seventy-two days. Something had to be done!

So, we did what any fine upstanding neighbor would do—we complained to city hall. The police came out and had Frank move the motor home, but instead of being the end of the difficulties, it was only the beginning. Frank was mad, really mad, and in hindsight I don't blame him, although he was clearly in violation of the code. I'm sure he was embarrassed and wondered why we didn't just come over and talk to him about it. We didn't, and it was obvious by his angry stares and body language that we were no longer on the "good neighbors" list. A few weeks later, he parked the motor home across from our driveway again, but walked over and said, "It will only be here today. We're going on a trip tomorrow." With that, he spun on his heels and walked back to his house. There were no pleasantries, no smiles, no well wishes, nothing.

Frank and his wife were gone for almost four months. I thought about them on more than one occasion and wished for a do-over. I can't say that I missed the motor home, but I felt bad about the way it all went down, and I missed his smile and friendly wave. I resolved that I would make amends as soon as they returned from their trip. Then one afternoon when I returned from the university, the motor home was back in its usual spot. I walked across the street but I couldn't find anyone to talk to. When I came into the house, Lori asked me what I was doing across the street, fearing that I was about to threaten to call the police again. "No," I said, "I went over to apologize. I feel bad about the way we handled the situation the last time." Lori smiled and said, "No need. As soon as they came home, I went over to talk with Frank. He saw me coming, threw up his arms, and promised to move the motor home by the end of the day. I said that that wasn't the reason for my visit. I wanted to apologize to him for calling the police before we talked to him. That wasn't the kind of neighbor I wanted to be. I stuck out my hand, said that I was sorry, and asked him to forgive me. Frank shook my hand and said, 'You bet!' That was it. The tension was gone."

Six months later, Lori graduated from seminary and I threw a little party to mark the occasion, inviting some of her close friends and seminary colleagues to celebrate with us. Lori invited Frank and his wife, too. Although I appreciated the gesture, I seriously doubted that they would come since they didn't know anyone else on the guest list, but come they did. I still have a vivid memory of Frank sitting in the middle of a group of Lori's friends, laughing and celebrating with her, and as he left, looking her squarely in the eyes and telling her that he was very proud of her. I was very proud of her, too. I still am.

* * *

These two stories have something in common—it is rarely easy to apologize and say you're sorry, and especially so when it seems that it isn't really our fault or at least when it isn't *all* our fault. Pride is the great inhibitor, a self-justifying deceiver, keeping us from doing what we know to be right, insisting that we have done nothing wrong. Yet deep within us, the Holy Spirit is speaking, too, telling us that something is out of tune, not right. When we listen to that still small voice, we know that something has to be done. And when we swallow our pride and eat some humble pie, it is grace that nourishes us—and restoration comes. These are sacred moments.

The Great Inhibitor of Grace

Pride is the great inhibitor, keeping us from humility's path that leads to grace and spiritual growth. It keeps us from hearing and responding to that still small voice urging humble action and prevents us from doing the very things that bring healing and hope in the midst of anger and hurt. I am convinced that there are no instant actions or quick ways to develop humility; it is a path to be walked.

Along the way, however, there are four simple, honest, humble, spiritual practices that keep pride in its place: saying I'm sorry, I was wrong, I need your help, and I don't know. John Ruskin thought that pride was at the bottom of all great mistakes. Certainly, I have come to believe that honestly and consistently saying these things will set one on humility's path, but be warned, there are no shortcuts. For most of us, it's a lifelong journey, not a day hike.

I'm Sorry

As the two preceding stories illustrate, saying "I'm sorry. Will you forgive me?" are two of the most disarming and healing statements we can ever make, and I believe it is true *even if the other person does not respond in a graceful manner*—even if they give you a piece of their mind instead of a handshake. Remember, it is our pride that we are dealing with. How someone responds to our apology is up to them; that's not our battle.

Remember also that our pride can skew how we see things and remember things, inhibiting restorative responses because pride sees only what others have done and causes amnesia when it comes to our own attitudes and actions. As provost at several Christian universities, I have had the onerous task of moderating personal disputes between two faculty members. Honestly, I can't even remember how often I have heard, "I am not going to apologize for anything because I have done *nothing* wrong." And sadly, in almost every case, I heard the same words from both individuals. There were frustrations, anger, and hurt—and no one did anything wrong—not a thing. Go figure. That's prideful blindness, and it is never helpful.

I Was Wrong

Sometimes it is not an apology but a do-over that is called for. During the first year of service as the provost at a university in the Southern Plains, I wrote a new strategic plan for the academic sector, complete with a revised vision and mission statement. I was out of town during the next scheduled faculty meeting, so I asked one of the deans to present the new plan for formal approval, needing a vote of at least 51 percent of the faculty. When I returned, the dean reported that there was good news and bad news. The good news was that the faculty approved the new plan and mission statement by a vote of 60 percent (they wanted to show support for the new provost); the bad news was that no one was very happy—not about the contents of the plan per se, but about the lack of consultation and process that went into its development.

I called a special all-faculty meeting the next day and began by saying that while I appreciated their affirmative vote, it was no way to run a university. I was wrong. Those who complained about having insufficient consultation and opportunities for input were absolutely correct, so I was asking for a do-over. I was setting aside the vote and starting over, and I outlined a detailed, transparent process that would give everyone an opportunity to speak into the development of the plan. A senior faculty member informed me that there were no provisions in the Faculty Handbook to set aside a faculty vote, and no history of a do-over. I said that there should be, and there would be now! The faculty agreed to the do-over, and the revised plan passed with a 100 percent vote, breaking yet another long-standing faculty precedent. Faculties rarely speak with one mind, but on this day they did.

On another occasion, I was talking to someone who was working in physical plant services. He told me that he started out as a pastor, but things went haywire in his first church when he proposed to sell the church and build a new one. There were heated discussions about his proposal and much division, but he felt he knew best, so he called for a vote of the entire church. The vote was 51 percent to 49 percent. He felt his leadership was on the line, so he declared that the move was God's will and moved ahead with plans to sell the existing church building. As you might suspect, this resulted in a nasty church split and the pastor was asked to leave. He never recovered and ended up leaving the ministry.

I asked him if he ever considered a do-over, to go back and start over, especially given such division and contention in the church. "No," he replied, "when God speaks, it is our job to listen and do his will. It's as simple as that. We have to fight the devil. My leadership was at stake and I'm proud of the way I led that church, even though it never recovered."

Even as a young professional, his prideful attitude struck me as misguided and quite sad. To this day, I wonder what might have happened in that church and in his ministry if he would have swallowed his pride, ate some humble pie, and honored the disagreement by asking for a do-over. It is a lesson I have never forgotten. When I hear someone say that their leadership is at stake, it is usually their pride that is in play. Admitting that we might be wrong and asking for a do-over is not a sign of weak leadership. Sadly, pride is the great inhibitor, making the truth hard to digest and grace hard to find.

Before we move on, there is one final comment that is in order. As I have suggested, saying *I was wrong* is difficult, but saying *You were right* can be even harder. And when you know that both are in play, it can turn into a double-feature pride drama. I've had to do both a time or two myself. It's not a lot of fun, to be sure, but it isn't fatal either. I guess sometimes the medicine goes down best in one big swallow.

I Need Your Help

A third spiritual practice that works against pride is simply admitting, first to ourselves and then to others, that we need help, that we can't do it all by ourselves. At the beginning of each doctoral class I taught over the years, I would give a speech that went something like this: "I know you take pride in being a doctoral student, but if you understand this simple concept, you will be much better off. There are persons in the library, skilled professionals, who have prepared their entire adult lives for you to come and simply say, 'I need your help.' As it turns out, it is one of the hardest things for a doctoral student to do. I think it has to do with the pride of being an advanced learner. And that you are, but asking for help will advance your learning in way that you can't even imagine. The journey to wisdom is a team sport, not a marathon."

I gave this speech at the beginning of every class because it usually took a few times to take hold. At some point or another, however, almost every student would drop by my office and admit that it was good advice, thanking me for the encouragement. And asking for help not only helps you, but it invites others to step up and get involved, too. It's a win-win. At the end of the day, true humility is a vision of community; pride is its great inhibitor.

I Don't Know

If it is hard for doctoral students to ask for help, and it is, it is even harder for young faculty members to admit that they don't know everything. College students often engage in a bit of hero worship of professors, and new teachers are unusually susceptible to it, probably because it is a new experience for them. Students put them on a pedestal, and professional pride keeps professors from being honest and admitting that their knowledge is actually quite limited, the very thing that students need to learn if they learn nothing else. Even the Apostle Paul admitted that he didn't know everything (1 Cor 13:12).

I would like to tell you that such professional pride is restricted to the academy, but of course it isn't. Sadly, it is at play in church leadership, both lay and clergy. I suspect that some of the difficulty to simply admit that we don't know everything comes from the influence of all-too-prominent podcasts on church leadership that insist that leaders must have answers, vision, and courage. Humility doesn't seem to sell as well, but when leaders admit that they don't have all the answers but look forward instead to finding answers together, it invites others to the table and allows leaders to climb down from their perch and take a seat at the table, too. Jesus said that the meek will inherit the earth (Matt 5:5). If this is so, perhaps the meek can lead effectively, too. Humility must be in play.

* * *

Pride is the great inhibitor. It keeps us from saying I'm sorry, I was wrong, I need your help, and I don't know—humble invitations all for forgiveness, restoration, growth, and grace. I believe that when the Apostle Paul wrote that *love is not proud*, he meant much the same thing.

Scripture

"When pride comes, then comes disgrace, but with humility comes wisdom" (Prov 11:2). There's no way for me to improve on the sage observations offered about pride and wisdom in this proverb, so let me just say "Amen" and offer two brief comments. First, as we have just seen, pride is the great inhibitor. It keeps us from humility's path and leaves us blind and deaf to opportunities to be real and vulnerable. Sadly, it is in these moments that healing comes and hope is restored. As it turns out, pride is an individual vice, while humility is a communal virtue.

Second, this proverb makes the connection between humility and wisdom. There is no such connection between pride and wisdom. In fact, pride is not only the great inhibitor of grace, it also inhibits spiritual growth, the pursuit of humility, and ultimately wisdom, too. So, are there concrete steps that we can take to pursue humility without becoming overly prideful about it? Thankfully, the answer is yes, and several Next Steps will follow.

Next Steps

I recently saw a commercial with a car racing down a deserted city street. Scrolling across the bottom of the screen were these words: *Professional driver on a closed course. Do not try this on your own.* That's good advice for all of us who desire to deal with pride. This can be a lifetime endeavor, so find some good traveling companions for the journey.

Ask For Help—Start At The Top

After Jesus cast out a spirit that robbed a young boy of speech, his disciples came to him in private and asked why they couldn't drive the spirit out. Apparently, they had tried and failed, probably in full public view. Jesus told them, "This kind can come out only by prayer" (Mark 9:29). Honestly, I'm not sure what Jesus meant by "this kind," but I think I think he meant that such healings were not a solo act, they required a deep connection with the Father, a spiritual connection—by prayer. It's not entirely clear but it seems that the disciples were focused more on the public aspects of the healings than on maintaining the spiritual connections that undergird them.

Inside the front cover of *Forward Day by Day,* a daily devotional published by the Episcopal Church, there is a prayer, *A Morning Resolve,* focused on the commitment to live a simple, sincere, and serene life. Near the end, the prayer calls attention to being faithful to the daily habits of prayer, work, study, physical exercise, eating, and sleep, and adds: "And as I cannot in my own strength do this, nor even with a hope of success attempt it, I look to thee, O God . . ." As the prayer clearly states, there are things that you simply cannot do by sheer will power. I think we can add dealing with pride to the list.

Jesus' words in Mark 9 and the words of *A Morning Resolve* remind us that the place to start when we want to see powerful change in our lives is with prayer—with a deep and constant connection to God. We work with God, not for God. We simply cannot do this alone, so ask for help. Start at the top. Invite the Holy Spirit to accompany you on the journey and lead your efforts as you go. Your job will be to listen and follow that still, small voice that provides both direction and hope.

Don't Just Stand There—Walk!

All too often, the solution we hear to any spiritual concern, whether it be pride, an addiction, or a troubled marriage, is to pray harder and read more Scripture. Please hear me—these are good things, but they are not, in and of themselves, the answer to all our problems. There are other concrete steps and practices that we can undertake that will reinforce our prayers and shape us in good ways, godly ways. Several have been mentioned in the previous section: saying I'm sorry, I was wrong, I don't know, and I need your help. There are others, of course, but start with these. Are there any apologies in order; any confessions; any admissions of shortcomings? Let the Holy Spirit prompt you, and when the promptings come, don't just stand there—walk! Give feet to your prayers.

Be Thankful

I was having coffee with a friend and talking about our life journeys, musing about how in the world two young kids, one from Minnesota and one from Michigan, ever found their way into their professions and ended up in a good place, retired in Oregon. In some ways, we agreed that the Way found us more than we found our way. I mentioned that it is easy to look back at my career and feel a deep sense of pride in my professional successes that could easily swell my head. My friend said that when he thinks about his career, he remembers all the persons who helped him along the way—parents, family, friends, neighbors, teachers, colleagues, and pastors, to name just a few. And when he does, he is grateful for their care and gives thanks. Looking at circumstances with gratitude works against a puffed-up sense of pride and self-importance. After all, none of us get to where we are all by ourselves. We stand on other's shoulders, but pride can cause amnesia.

So, be thankful. Be grateful. Make a gratitude list and review it often. Carry it with you. This is a great reminder that we are not self-made, and a reminder to take the opportunity to call or write someone, expressing gratitude for the way they have influenced your life. Be specific. I guarantee you that it will make their day, and it will do wonders for your day, too, keeping excessive pride at bay.

Conclusion

I'm not sure why the Apostle Paul included envy, boasting, and pride in the same sentence, but he did: "It [love] does not envy, it does not boast, it is not proud" (1 Cor 13:4b). Envy is an internal feeling, boasting is an external action or reaction, and pride is the great inhibitor. Pride is the nasty one that keeps us from responding to that still small voice that tells us that something is out of tune and needs to be addressed. It causes us to be spiritually deaf and blind, and prevents us from the humble acts of saying I am sorry, I was wrong, I don't know, I need your help, and I would like a do-over—the very portions of humble pie that allow grace to nourish us and to bring help, hope, and healing to the messes we make and face.

And as it turns out, dealing with pride is not a solo act. We start at the top, asking God to be with us, buttress our intentions, and guide our efforts, weak as they are. And as we attune our ears to the still small voice of the Holy Spirit, guidance and courage come. As we focus on being grateful rather than basking in our own glory, we come to understand that we all stand on the shoulders of others, and we have the opportunity to give someone else a boost, too. Through it all, humility will come as we are slowly, steadily, and surely shaped in the image of Christ, who was and is holy and humble.

For most of us, it is a lifelong journey, but it is also the journey of a lifetime.

Questions for Reflection and Discussion:

1. There is a fine line between being proud and having excessive pride. Is it a difficult line for you to navigate?

2. Why is pride in others so easy to spot and so difficult to deal with in our own lives?
3. What prevents us from willingly saying: "I was wrong. I'm sorry"? Does the culture of perfection (especially for those in church leadership of one kind or another) work against such humble acts?
4. What is the difference between being humiliated and being humble?
5. If you think about the shoulders of others that you stand on, who comes to mind? Have you told them so?

Love is patient, love is kind. It does not envy,
it does not boast, it is not proud. . . .

— 6 —

Love Does Not Dishonor Others

I've learned that people will forget what you said, people will forget what you did, but people will never forget how you made them feel.

—Maya Angelou

Introduction

Several translations simply state: love is not rude. That makes good sense. I was always taught to be courteous to everyone, whether I loved them or not. After all, we all want to be treated in a way that preserves our dignity and sense of well-being, and when we treat others in such a way, it preserves our own dignity, too. Truly, love is not rude, and being rude is no way to love anyone.

Other translations, including the NIV we are using in this book, put it this way: love does not dishonor others. This expands discourteous and disrespectful behaviors (being rude) to include those that shame, humiliate, and degrade (dishonoring others), clearly no way to love anyone. This, it seems to me, demands far more from us. Even in a messy situation, perhaps especially in a messy situation, love is not just about being respectful; it is also about being kind. Simply put, love does not dishonor others.

And in this chapter, I want to push our thinking about love a bit further still. If we take away the double negative from "love does not dishonor others," we are left with this, "love honors others." To me, this is radical Christianity, a truly hard teaching. Particularly in a mess, what if the standard of behavior was not simply to avoid being rude and dishonoring others, but to honor them? What if we didn't just take the slap on the face, we turned the other cheek (Matt 5:39)? What if we didn't just surrender our shirt, we gave away our coat, too (5:40)? And what if when we were required to carry someone's pack one mile, we carried it a second mile (5:41)? Could we actually do this? Do we have the strength, courage, and humility to live this way? Honestly, this is hard for me because I would rather slap back, take back, and get even, but these are the words of Jesus from the Sermon on the Mount (Matt 5–7).

If you agree with me that love asks us to honor others, and not just when we feel like it, we all have some work to do. So, let's start at the beginning and see where it takes us. I think we'll end up in a good but challenging place. This is as it should be. No one ever said that spiritual growth was for the faint of heart.

Love Is Not Rude

There is good reason for the Apostle Paul to remind the Corinthian congregation, a church in a mess, that love is not rude—offensively impolite, discourteous, and disrespectful of others. Honestly, it is a real temptation to be rude to those who brag, boast, envy, and expect to be put on a pedestal or demand to be treated with kid gloves, all the while treating others with a certain disrespect or disdain. Simply put, it is terribly hard to put up with those who lack basic social courtesies and a genuine respect for others. Our basic reflex is to return the favor, but when we do, we sink to the level of those we deplore.

Young children who are still learning about how to love others and themselves must work hard to harness their selfish emotions. They find it easy to be rude to other children—name calling, teasing, tattling, bullying, and disrespecting them for how they look or what clothes they wear. It is ugly to watch, as any elementary schoolteacher will attest, but Paul wasn't writing to children, although he most certainly was writing to adults who were acting like children. When a church is in a mess, respectful social discourse can easily go out the window, and it is replaced by behaviors that would garner any third grader a lecture and a time-out from the playground. Gossip flows, cliques form, and rude behavior carries the day, all in the name of loving each other and protecting the church. But as Paul clearly states, love is not rude. Surely, we are called to a higher standard than to act like rude children in church.

So, rude is simply out, but as we will see, dishonoring others is even worse. It's rudeness with a nasty edge. We'll take up this all too familiar practice next.

PART II: LOVE OUT OF BOUNDS

Love Does Not Dishonor Others

Love does not dishonor others. What a pointed and powerful statement, abundantly clear, needing little explanation. No room for ambiguity—if you dishonor others, it isn't in the name of love; and since we are called to love both God and our neighbors as ourselves, it is way out of bounds. To dishonor someone is to discredit, humiliate, degrade, give a bad name or drag it through the mud, to bring shame or disgrace. It is easy to see that these are not loving actions.

When a church is in a mess, dishonoring behavior takes many forms, but it seems to me the big three are hurt feelings, gossip, and poor theology. I'm not sure why people get their feelings hurt over such small things, but they do. They aren't asked to sing a solo or give the announcements. They aren't asked to lead the prayer team or coordinate the entire women's discipleship conference, even though they are asked to play a key role in the event. They don't feel that they are publicly recognized or thanked enough for their efforts. It seems that such persons are not just fragile, they come on the lookout for a reason to get their feelings hurt and take it out on others. And when they do, the drama begins—they complain, they criticize, they denounce, and they gossip—boy, do they gossip, and they enlist others to do their bidding, too. It is an infectious activity, and it can take on a life of its own, sustaining itself with venom and unkindness. They dishonor others out of their own feelings of inadequacy and wounded pride, and tear away at the fabric of the community, destroying its integrity like a swarm of termites attacking an old shed. Simply put, love doesn't act that way.

The theology police in any congregation are a special case. They don't act out of a sense of wounded pride or slight. It might be better if they did. Rather, they are on a mission, acting with an all-too-holy certainty, working in subtle and not so subtle ways to run off or stifle or discredit anyone who thinks or believes differently from them. After all, they have the Truth, all of it. They dishonor others in an attempt to protect God from bad theology. As it turns out, they are often the purveyors of bad theology themselves. Dishonoring others who believe or read Scripture differently is no way to defend or honor the God of the universe. In fact, it is poor theology to do so.

Fragile feelings, gossip, and poor theology kill the spirit and work against the work of the Holy Spirit in our midst. So, what can be done? Before we look to Scripture and offer a few "Next Steps," let's consider an approach that will require a total reframe of our view of a messy situation and will demand all the kindness and humility we can muster—maybe more. Thankfully, we do not do this in our own strength alone. Thanks be to God.

Love Honors Others

It is one thing to avoid dishonoring someone, but it is an altogether different thing to honor someone, particularly those who have a shadow side or seem to take particular joy in promoting themselves and their achievements. It is not simply a next step; it is a long walk, a second mile.

One of my joys as a provost (a fancy title for the chief academic officer at a university) was serving as convener and moderator for faculty meetings. It is true that such meetings with persons trained to be critical thinkers and more than willing to share their opinions are known to be rambunctious at times, but honestly, I loved the give and take. I started each meeting with the Candy Bar Award. I would call forward a faculty member or two and highlight something that had come to my attention—something like taking a group of students to a regional conference or accepting an extra task (usually thankless) in their department or receiving a positive affirmation from a student or parent. And I would give them a chocolate candy bar and ask the faculty to honor them with some applause. They always did.

At first, the honorees were caught off-guard and seemed a bit embarrassed. I usually received a note or two later in the week saying that while such notice of their work was appreciated, it was totally unnecessary—and they usually reported on the fate of the candy bar. Often it didn't make it back to the office, and if it did, it was shared with their kids that evening.

In the second year of the Candy Bar Awards, things began to change. I would receive notes from honorees indicating that the candy bar was now displayed proudly on the corner of their desk or on a bookshelf for all to see. One even had the candy bar framed and mounted on display right behind her desk for all to see. And by the third year, I would receive notes from faculty members listing out their activities for the month and wondering if that would merit an award. The candy bar now had symbolic significance!

I'll let you in on a little secret. I started giving away candy bars as a way of recognizing and reinforcing faculty activities that I thought would help us offer a deeper and more formative educational experience for our students. That worked, to be sure, but I was not expecting how powerful such a simple act of honoring someone could be, even crusty, cantankerous, seasoned professors.

I've come to believe that honoring someone is a humble act, a formative sacred act, and sadly when a church is in a mess, honor and honoring go out the window at the very time when such activities are most needed. There is power in regarding someone with respect and showing appreciation, and particularly so when we know about that person's shadow side. That doesn't need to cancel the honor, and that's good news for all of us because we have a shadow side, too, and if we are honest, we wouldn't mind a bit of recognition coming our way. At the end of the day, encouragement and recognition cost nothing, but mean everything. Love honors others, and not just when we feel like it.

Scripture

While growing up, my brothers and I heard on more than one occasion that it was not only good to honor our father and mother, it was one of the ten commandments—the Law (Exod 20:12a; Deut 5:16). We had to! At the time, I'm sure that we didn't catch the full meaning of the commandment, but we caught enough to know that honoring our parents meant that we were to do as we were told without sassing back or acting out in public, and if we disobeyed we would really catch it—and "it" was something to be avoided! Certainly, there was a price to be paid for rude or dishonoring behavior.

Over time, however, honoring my parents or anyone else for that matter began to take on a richer meaning. It wasn't simply doing what I was told or living up to their expectations, but intentionally highlighting their accomplishments and recurring calendar events like birthdays and anniversaries. It was a way of "seeing" them and expressing gratitude for the quality of their lives and for their investment in my own. I honored them by paying attention to them.

My parents are now gone, and it is only now that I am coming to understand the full biblical meaning of honoring. There is, of course, a sense of obedience, celebration, and remembrance in honoring them, but there is also a sense of giving them weight and influence in the way that I live my life—even now. It allows me to honor my parents long after they are gone, and I do. They continue to influence my life—my outlook, my vision, and my values, and as I give them weight, I honor them.

Of course, I honor others, too, past and present—my professors, my mentors, my close friends, my pastor, my wife, and Dallas Willard—by giving weight to what they think (or thought), what they say (or said), what they value (or valued), what they believe (or believed), and how they live (or lived). This brings a deeper dimension to the idea of honoring others. It is one thing to avoid behaving rudely or dishonoring others, but it is another thing altogether to honor others, to give them weight. It is ultimately an expression of profound love, and honoring others serves as a good reminder that we do not journey alone. Community is the soil for deep spiritual growth.

In what follows, we will look at several examples from Scripture where Jesus gave weight to others, and as we will see, the honorees are not always the high and mighty or the chair of the church board. Hopefully, there is a lesson in this for all of us who claim Christ, even in the midst of the mess that we call the church.

Jesus and John the Baptizer[1]

No one knows for sure why John the Baptizer sent two of his followers to question Jesus about his activities and intentions, but send them he did (Matt 11:3; Luke 7:18–26). John was sitting in Herod's prison, his own future quite uncertain. No doubt he was alone, afraid, discouraged, and perhaps disillusioned, but why did he worry about Jesus? Did he have doubts that Jesus was the Messiah? Was he worried that he had prepared the way for the wrong person? Was he concerned that Jesus was going about his mission all wrong? Was Jesus too passive? Was he misguided? Did John want to see more action? Honestly, we do not know, but we do know that John's two disciples came to Jesus early in his ministry and on behest of John asked this question in full public view, "Are you the one who is to come, or should we expect someone else?" (Luke 7:19). Wow, what a rude question from a family member and key supporter, a sting to be sure.

It seems to me that Jesus had every right and reason to be indignant. After all, wasn't John's mother, Elizabeth, one of the first to know of Jesus' coming birth? Didn't Mary and Elizabeth spend months together? Didn't they talk about the visit of the angel? Wasn't John's father visited by an angel, too? And didn't John baptize Jesus in the Jordan River, seeing the Spirit descend upon him like a dove and hearing the voice of God affirm his identity? Did he forget all their history, all that they had been through together?

Jesus could have easily and understandably been rude, giving John's disciples a piece of his mind and sending them away. After all, they were questioning not only his calling and his ministry, but also his very identity—and doing so in public. It could have been an ugly scene, but it wasn't. Rather, Jesus told his questioners to go back to John and report what they had witnessed: the blind receiving their sight, the lame walking . . . and good news preached to the poor (Luke 7:22). Surely, John would have recognized that this response had the fingerprints of the prophet Isaiah all over it (Isa 35:5), and he would have been satisfied. That could have been the end of

---

1. Much of this reflection about Jesus and John first appeared in Patrick Allen, *For Today: A Prayer When Life Gets Messy* (Eugene, OR: Cascade, 2018), 94–95. Used by permission.

the confrontation, John's disciples turned away with a kind and hopeful response with no dishonor or disrespect extended, but that wasn't the end of it. Jesus then turned to the crowd of listeners and talked to them about John the Baptist, the one who had just questioned his identity and ministry, or at least his tactics as the coming messiah. He praised and affirmed John, telling the crowd that he was a prophet and a good one, and much more. He was a forerunner, and one of the best persons he knew. Instead of dishonoring John, he affirmed and honored him. To me, that was grace in action. After all, love honors others.

Zacchaeus and Judas

Zacchaeus and Judas are not the most popular names for new babies these days, and for good reason. Jesus could have easily dishonored both men, one for being a tax collector, a traitor to his people, and the other for plotting with the Jewish leaders, a traitor to the Cause. Yet Jesus chose to honor them instead. Honestly, it is hard to understand.

Jesus was making his way through Jericho, intent on heading on down the road, when he spotted Zacchaeus sitting on a tree limb behind the crowd (Luke 19:1–10). Jesus immediately changed his plans, asked Zacchaeus to come down, and invited himself and his companions for dinner. The onlookers were stunned! "Isn't Zacchaeus a despised traitor, a sinner?" they mumbled to each other, loud enough for everyone to hear. The answer, of course, was yes and yes, and that seems to be exactly why Jesus went out of his way and went to his house for dinner. He honored Zacchaeus, giving him weight. In the end, Zacchaeus promised to make restitution and change his ways, which as far as we know he did. But even if he didn't, Jesus made it clear that Zacchaeus was as much a child of Abraham as the rest of them (19:9). Maybe that was the point, a stunning way of honoring Zacchaeus, backing up his words that he came to seek and save the lost (19:10). Love does not dishonor others; it welcomes them.

The story of Judas is even more striking. On the night Jesus was betrayed, he took his disciples to an upstairs room for a Passover meal. All four Gospels record aspects of this event (Matt 26:17–30; Mark 14:12–26; Luke 22:7-38; John 13:1–30). Jesus washed their feet, served them bread and wine, and gave them a glimpse into the events that were about to unfold. It wasn't a happy picture. Luke even tells us that in the midst of this sadness, a dispute arose as to which disciple was the greatest (22:24), presumably arguing about who would take over the mantle of leadership of the movement if Jesus' predictions came true. Sad timing, indeed.

Christians remember this "last supper" every time they participate in the Eucharist. What is not always remembered is that even though Jesus knew Judas was up to no good, Jesus invited him to the table, washed his feet, and served him, *like all the others*. He honored Judas in the hours just before he was about to go to his own hideous death.

Honestly, I don't get it. Perhaps Jesus was trying to make Judas feel guilty, giving Judas one last chance to call a halt to his plans and turn from his wicked ways. Perhaps he was trying to show all of us that Judas wasn't much different from the rest of us, if at all, or maybe he was just honoring him for no particular reason other than the fact that he was there and in as much need of love and care as anyone else. I really don't know, but I do know that Jesus could have told Judas to stay away or wait outside, but instead offered him a seat at the table of the most poignant and celebrated dinner ever recorded in human history. In the midst of pain and turmoil and betrayal, Love chose to honor others. I think there's a lesson in this for all of us.

Next Steps

I trust we agree with the Apostle Paul that love is not rude, nor does it dishonor others. And I hope you agree with me that love can honor others, even when we would rather be in the limelight ourselves. That's a natural human response, of course, but not the kingdom way of doing business. So how do we avoid being rude and dishonoring, and learn to honor others? Here are some next steps for the journey.

Rude Is Crude

At best, rude is crude. When we encounter rude behavior, particularly in the church, there are several things to keep in mind. First, don't be surprised. I wish it were different, but rude and nasty behavior exists, even seems to thrive in congregations of all sizes. Recently I heard of someone who would not even look at a particular person at church, let alone speak to them, and this was in a church of less than one hundred members where both had attended for years—and had known each other for most of their lives. How sad! Getting or giving the silent treatment is just plain rude, but it happens, and it happens in church.

So, don't be surprised, and don't respond in kind, although that is often our first reaction. It's quite human to fight back. In the end, however, it only multiplies the difficulties and puts us in the middle of the skirmish. Rather than returning a rude response, just walk away. That is, put some distance between you and that person or group, and take some time to reflect about what triggered their actions and what might be driving such rude behavior. Usually there's a long story behind such behavior—you're only the latest casualty, not the only one.

Then, seek out someone who is both safe and discerning, and try to figure out the best way to respond, if at all. In some instances, it is such a messy situation that the best way forward is simply to keep your distance and practice patience and kindness. At other times, especially if others are being hurt by such behavior, some type of intervention is in order. I know of no rule as to when we should confront the rude person ourselves or when we should seek help from others. The key, I believe, is to minimize the storm, but to be sure that rude behavior is addressed in a kind but forthright way. Rude behavior is rarely a one-time event. If it isn't challenged early on, it can take on a life of its own, and sadly, it can become normative behavior for the congregation. When that happens, rude behavior will surely replicate. Since we know that love is not rude, and it is the practice of love that is central to a healthy congregation, rude behavior must be ruled out of bounds.

Dealing with Dishonor

If rude behavior is out of bounds, surely actions and attitudes that dishonor anyone are far worse, and when they are aimed directly at us, the first response is fight or flight. Sometimes we want to do both at the same time. As with rude behavior, it takes discernment to know when and how to respond, if at all. It seems to me that each situation needs to be addressed in view of its own unique circumstances with grace and courage and hope. The key is to keep our focus on our own integrity, something that no one can take from us, and to live in such a way that those who try to dishonor us will not be believed. (In addition, the challenges of letting go, moving on, and forgiving are addressed in detail in chapter 9.)

Honoring Others

Perhaps the best corrective for rude and dishonorable behavior is to intentionally honor others. It can be as simple as counteracting gossip or complaints about the pastor's sermon or the music leader's choice of music by saying something you really admire about that person. This usually stops gossip and complaining in their tracks. If it does, fine. If it doesn't, then just repeat step one until it does. You'll find that those who complain and gossip need a willing and supportive listener. Just don't be one.

One last comment about honoring others, especially those who have influenced your life. Remember them—make a list, and then let them know the influence they have had on your life. Be specific. I promise that even a simple note or conversation over a cup of coffee with be remembered and relished for a lifetime. It will cost you practically nothing, but it will mean everything to them. And finally, live it forward. That is to say, remember those who have influenced your life in a good way, tell them so, and then live so that your life will give weight to others in the same way. Live it forward as an expression of gratitude and hope. You will not be disappointed.

Conclusion

Whether 1 Corinthians 13:5 is translated into English as rude or dishonorable behavior, the Apostle Paul is clear that love doesn't behave that way. We often excuse rude behavior as just being impolite, but it is much more dangerous and damaging to a congregation than that. In fact, there is no place in the church for behaviors that are offensively impolite, discourteous, and disrespectful of others. It divides, diminishes, and destroys community, and saps the human spirit. It is simply out of bounds.

And if rude behavior is out of bounds, little more needs to be said about actions and attitudes that dishonor others. Behaviors that discredit, humiliate, and degrade others are no way to love anyone—way out of bounds. Those of us who claim Christ must live to a much higher standard—to love God with all we have and are, and to love our neighbors as if our communal life depended on it. In many ways, I think it does. Love does not dishonor others.

At the end of the day, perhaps the best way to combat rude behavior is to avoid entering into the fray, as tempting as it may be to do so. Then, to carefully and prayerfully find ways to make it clear that such behaviors are unacceptable because they tear at the heart of the body of Christ, and then nip any subsequent behavior in the bud. Quick and kind corrections are much easier and less painful than major interventions.

And finally, we can all be role models by honoring others, recognizing and honoring those who have weight and influence in our lives. Finding ways to express such gratitude is a powerful reminder that we don't journey alone. It is also a good way to set an example and to remind others that love is not rude. In fact, honoring others is a sacred act.

Questions for Reflection and Discussion:

1. Why do you think that rude behavior thrives so easily in messy church communities?
2. Have you ever been given or witnessed the "silent treatment" in church? What was the result of this type of shunning?
3. Who were or are the major influences in your own spiritual walk? How have you given them weight?
4. What might you do to express gratitude to these honorees?
5. What does it mean for you to honor forward? How might you "live it forward" as mentioned at the end of "Next Steps"?

Love is patient, love is kind. It does not envy, it does not boast, it is not proud. It does not dishonor others . . .

— 7 —

Love Is Not Self-Seeking

*He did not fail to confess, but confessed freely,
"I am not the Messiah."*

—John 1:20

Introduction

Love is not self-seeking, Paul tells us in 1 Corinthians 13:5, or as the NRSV puts it, "Love does not insist on its own way." As it turns out, self-seeking or insisting on our own way is no way to serve or minister to anyone, and when the church is in a mess, it just adds to the mess or creates a mess of its own. It is a multiplier!

In this chapter, I'll share several vignettes where self-seeking took on a life of its own before we look at several forms of self-seeking in the mess and what can be done to promote kindness and patience instead. I think a good place to start is to join John the Baptizer in affirming, "I am not the Messiah" (John 1:20). The good news for all of us is that that assignment has already been taken. Thanks be to God.

Self-Seeking Stories

The following vignettes are drawn from my own experience. I wish I could tell you that I made them up, but I didn't. They are both sad and funny, each in their own way, but true, and if we are honest, we might find a bit of our own selves in them, too. It seems to me that none of us are immune from self-seeking behaviors at one time or another. The key is to avoid making it a habit or the default approach to every situation we encounter. I will suggest some

Next Steps later in the chapter to deal with our own self-seeking, but first let me introduce you to some personalities you may already know.

Sally Saves the Circus and Ruins Thanksgiving

One year while away at college, I was invited to a friend's home for Thanksgiving. When we arrived, the house was decorated in Thanksgiving splendor—pumpkins, bouquets of flowers, and a hand-crafted cornucopia centerpiece that overflowed with gourds, ears of corn, apples, and grapes. As I stood gazing at all the decorations, my friend leaned over and said to me, "Mom does all the decorating. We're not allowed to help or touch anything." That comment seemed a bit strange to me, but I would soon find out that that wasn't the only thing that his mom did on her own. In fact, she did *everything* on her own.

She started early Thanksgiving morning in the kitchen, wearing a light blue bathrobe, a fluffy pair of white slippers, and a headband. It was quite a sight. When I asked if I could help in any way, she told me that the best way to help was to stay out of her way. That I did, but it felt strange because at home we all pitched in to help out as best we could. She worked furiously most of the day, working up a full sweat (I now understood why she was wearing a headband), and by four o'clock the long dining room table and the two side tables were filled with so much food that I wondered if the entire neighborhood was joining us. We all stood behind our assigned seats for the Thanksgiving prayer. All of us were dressed up for the occasion except for my friend's mother, who stood there in her morning garb, sweating profusely and breathing heavily. As soon as the prayer was offered and we took our seats, she announced that she was simply too tired to join us and went to her bedroom to rest.

During the meal, family members took turns going to her bedside to thank her for all her hard work. I was even asked if I wanted to go and visit, but I declined. After dinner, I started to clear the table but was told that she had her own way of doing the cleanup, so it was better for all concerned to just go outside and play flag football. That we did.

Honestly, it all felt very strange, and it seemed to me that the family went along with the drama, playing their parts in allowing the matriarch to run the show and upstage the occasion in a heroic attempt to do everything. Somehow, the only gratitude expressed at the Thanksgiving meal was for all the hard work she had done. The reason for getting together in the first place was sadly lost. In an attempt to save the circus, she spoiled the celebration—turning the occasion into a self-seeking, self-centered tragedy.

It's All About Me—A Self-Serving Leader

Three faculty members came to my office to complain about their department chair. It seemed that he was personally doing the academic advising for their fifty students—all of them, causing long lines and delays in scheduling, and even though they offered, even insisted on helping out, he politely refused and offered this explanation: "This is my area of expertise and I don't need any help."

When the department chair and I met for a visit, I asked him why he didn't share the academic advising load with his departmental colleagues, and he simply insisted that he was the best advisor on campus, and he enjoyed meeting with each student. I pointed out the frustration felt by both his students and his colleagues, and I told him that when I was in college, even though I was the best shooter on the basketball team, I didn't take every shot. If I tried, it would wear me out and demoralize my teammates. He needed to share the load, and he said he would.

The next semester, he did share the load—well, at least a little. He assigned one advisee to each of his colleagues and kept forty-seven for himself. At best, it was the least he could do, so we had another talk. This time, he broke into tears as he shared that advising was what gave him significance on campus and made him feel important—a hero. I understood, having guessed the reason for his hoarding behavior. I pointed out that he was misusing his power as department chair, frustrating students, and limiting his colleagues' involvement in an important academic process. Simply put, it wasn't a good educational model and it worked against the desire of the faculty for each student to have a personal and meaningful relationship with their academic advisor. Too many students felt that they were being treated like cattle, and at the end of the day, it was all so he could feel better about himself. Such self-serving behavior had to stop.

The next semester, at my insistence the advising loads were evenly distributed among the faculty, and the advising process was much better—lasting only two days instead of two weeks. Everyone was pleased with the process except the department chair. He started telling other department chairs that I had overstepped my authority and ruined his work at the university. Shortly thereafter, he resigned his leadership position, insisting that all the fun of leading was gone. Honestly, his colleagues didn't object, and no one asked him to reconsider. Such self-seeking behavior is no way to lead or love anyone.

This is MY Ministry

I would like to tell you that self-seeking behavior is limited to family holidays and academic departments, but sadly it is all too common in our churches, especially in the midst of a mess. I recently heard of a music leader at a small church who wouldn't allow any suggestions from the worship team. If someone suggested a different song or simply asked a question about how to sing a certain phrase or to confirm the order of the service, he would angrily proclaim that *he* was in charge and they were mere volunteers, so their job was to simply do what he told them to do without any questions or suggestions. He was in charge and this was *his* ministry.

Needless to say, morale suffered, and some volunteers decided that they would rather work in the nursery. When the pastor asked them why they were no longer singing, they told him, and when he confronted the music leader about his treatment of the volunteers, he wrote a letter to the church board and district office complaining that the pastor was on a power trip and frustrating *his* ministry. When no one agreed with him, he resigned in a huff and moved out of state, leaving the church in a lurch. Several years later, he wrote to the district leadership, wondering if they might want him to come back and resume *his* ministry among them. They didn't, and politely said so.

* * *

Sadly, you have probably experienced similar episodes. I don't know why so many self-seekers are oblivious to the negative impact they have on others. They think that they are being heroic, but their desperate attempts to receive approval, applause, and affirmation result in just the opposite. They find themselves ignored and isolated, and when that happens the typical response is anger, recrimination, and often an ungracious exit. No wonder the Apostle Paul underscored that love is not self-seeking. As it turns out, self-seeking in no way to love anyone. It is hard on relationships, snaking its way in and through the congregation, turning service into tribute and people into pawns.

Self-Seeking

A friend of mine was the main speaker in a university chapel service, and for his sermon he quoted the Sermon on the Mount (Matt 5–8) from memory. When we finished, he simply left the podium and sat down. After the service, several students came to him, wondering why he didn't say more about the passage. "Is that all?" they asked, "Why didn't you preach from the passage?" My friend responded by saying that he didn't think any more needed to be said, that Jesus' words spoke for themselves.

When the Apostle Paul wrote to the congregation in Corinth and told them that love is not self-seeking, I feel like saying the same thing—the words speak for themselves (but that would make for a very short chapter). Intuitively we all get it. Self-seeking behavior is not only irritating, it is also unhealthy, eventually sapping the energy and spirit of the congregation while diminishing its capacity to identify and develop others for service and leadership. Just look at the synonyms for self-seeking: egocentric, self-absorbed, self-centered, self-infatuated, self-preoccupied, self-promoting, conceited, pompous, self-glorifying, self-indulgent, smug, egotistical, greedy, mercenary, constantly needing validation and reassurance. If these words do not convince you that self-seeking behaviors are detrimental, there is little else that I can say. Simply put, self-seeking works against the well-being of any faith community, no matter how well-intentioned. The church needs servants, not heroes.

The Needy Performance Trio

Approval, applause, and affirmation are not bad things in and of themselves, of course. We all appreciate a word of encouragement or some well-deserved recognition from time to time, but for the self-seeker, they can easily become a needy performance trio. That is, they fuel behaviors that constantly beg affirmation and positive answers to self-seeking questions: Am I doing it right? Did I do it right? Do they like me? Do you like me? Incessant self-seekers live for the fleeting high that comes from the attention they receive from others, but sadly the shelf life is extremely limited. It can even become an addiction, and social media makes it worse by telling us all the time, in "real" time, how many followers we have and how many like our posts, as if the more we have makes us special in some way. Social media provides instant gratification, but we surrender our self-worth into the hands of others who live in a fantasy land. That's not a prescription for developing deep personal relationships and living a grounded abundant life. And as we shall see, self-seeking has a way of thriving when the church is in a mess, too, and if we are honest, that is most of our churches at one time or another—or even now.

Forms of Self-Seeking in a Messy Congregation

Self-seeking often shows up in a messy congregation through the actions of the *circus-saver*, someone who jumps in to help out anywhere needed, and initially the help is greatly appreciated. But over time, much like the department head who wouldn't let anyone else advise students or the mother who would prepared the entire Thanksgiving meal without any assistance, it becomes a solo act as they drive anyone away who offers to help. They save the circus, but the circus become their personal jurisdiction, and when that happens, others are robbed of opportunities to serve. And at the same time, the capacity of the organization to respond effectively to the growing needs around them is diminished, even curtailed. What starts out as a welcome offer to jump in and help out sadly becomes a controlling, power-grabbing form of self-seeking. Certainly, that's not the way to love your church, even if it is in a mess.

A second form of self-seeking is the *spotlight seeker*, someone who is always willing, always pushing, even desperate, to be up front—to be seen. While serving as a greeter at a local church, I have had individuals offer to lead the prayer team, give the announcements, shepherd the senior adults ministries, sing in the music team, and even fill in for the pastor on a Sunday morning—and it was their first time to visit the church! They said that they just wanted to be a blessing and help out in any way they could, but I had the strong suspicion that it had more to do with their own sense of self-seeking rather than any sense of helping out, regardless of how needy the situation was. Ironically, I have yet to receive an offer from anyone to help with the coffee, set up and put away the chairs, or pick up the signs after the meeting. It seems that spotlighting and service are two different skill sets.

One final form of self-seeking bears mentioning—the *validation needer*—someone who is constantly needing assurance and seeking validation and forgiveness, regardless of the nature of the task. Did I sing okay? Are the bulletins printed and folded properly? Did I speak too often in the committee meeting? Do they like me? And along with a raft of self-serving questions, there is an overwhelming flood of apologies—I'm sorry that I was late. I apologize for interrupting. I'm sorry that I forgot about the meeting on Saturday. I'm sorry, I'm sorry, I'm sorry. After a while, the constant need for validation and forgiveness drains the energy from leaders and followers alike.

Honestly, I am not sure why such self-seeking behaviors—the circus saver, the spotlight seeker, and the validation needer—so easily emerge and flourish in a messy situation, but sadly they do. And I am not sure why such behaviors are so obvious to almost everyone, yet totally unrecognizable to the self-seeker. Somehow such behavior causes a sort of perceptual blindness. So, what can be done when we encounter self-seeking among those who claim Christ, or we come to the realization that we are self-seekers, too? In the Next Steps section below, we will look at some strategies for dealing with self-seeking, but first let's look to several passages from Scripture for wisdom and insight. Suffice it here to say that Paul spoke from experience and with good reason when he wrote to the messy Corinthian church—love is not self-seeking. He was spot on.

Scripture

There are two particular passages about self-seeking that I think are excellent examples for us—one from the Old Testament where self-seeking almost ruined the opportunity for healing and restoration, and one from the New Testament that gives insight into how to counteract self-seeking even before it raises its ugly head. I hope they are both instructive.

Naaman (2 Kings 5)

Naaman, we are told, was commander of the army of the king of Aram, widely known as a valiant fighter, and highly respected by his boss, the king—but he had leprosy. At that time and in that place, leprosy was both physically and socially lethal. Through the advice of a slave girl and with the assistance of his king, however, Naaman made his way first to the king of Israel, and then to Elisha, with hopes of being healed. He came prepared to give away tons of gold and ten sets of clothing, both as a way of expressing thankfulness to anyone who could heal him *and* as a way of demonstrating his own importance. As it turns out, it was probably more the latter than the former. Elisha didn't even come to the door to acknowledge Naaman or receive his gifts, but merely sent a messenger to tell Naaman to go to the Jordan River and wash himself seven times. That would do the trick.

According the Scripture, "Naaman went away angry" (5:11). Think about it for a minute. Nathan was offered healing from a dreaded and lethal disease, but stomped away in anger because he wasn't received with pomp and circumstance and treated like someone special. Sadly, he forgot why he was there in the first place.

Thankfully cooler heads prevailed. Naaman did eventually go and wash himself in the river, and he was healed of his leprosy. I do give Naaman high marks for listening to his faithful servants who confronted him about his embarrassing, self-serving behavior, most likely at great risk, and for the humility to follow Elisha's simple instructions. May we all have faithful ones who journey with us and call us out when we stomp away in anger, and may we have the humility to adjust course midstream when healing and restoration are offered to us. It seems that humility and healing often go hand in hand. We rarely get to do things on our own terms.

John the Baptist (John 1:19–28)

The Gospel of John is written in a more reflective style than the other Gospels, and the writer seems to have little interest in Jesus' lineage or the miracles that surrounded his birth. Rather, he begins his Gospel in poetic fashion with a reflection on how the Word became flesh, dwelling among us in grace and truth (1:1–14), and then moves quickly to the ministry and testimony of John the Baptist at Bethany on the other side of the Jordan River. Here some priests and Levites confront John with a direct question, "Are you the Messiah?" John responds, "*I am not the Messiah*" (1:19–20). They then wonder if he might be Elijah or the Prophet. Again, same answer, "*No*" (v. 21). When pressed for his identity, John simply quotes the words of Isaiah, "I am the voice of one calling in the wilderness, Make straight the way of the Lord" (v. 23).

I love this passage for several reasons. First, John knew who he wasn't—I am not the Messiah, not Elijah, and not the Prophet. No, he confessed freely, "This is not me." I think it is important for all of us who claim Christ to understand that we are not the Messiah or Elijah or the Prophet, as tempting as such roles may be from time to time. We are the branches, not the vine, as Jesus tells us in John 15:5.

It is also important to note that John knew who he was and what he was called to do—I am the voice. And not only did John know who he was and what he was called to do, he went out and did it. No one could stop him, even if it would cost him his very life—and eventually it did. No self-serving behavior here, just pure love.

Next Steps

Our Own Self-Seeking

We would all like to focus on the self-seeking behavior in others, but let's start a little closer to home—with our own. If we know we are prone to self-seeking or someone close to us points it out, what do we do? What can we do? The place to start, I believe, is to deal honestly with our efforts to shine in the spotlight, save the circus, or seek validation at every turn. Where does this need come from? What spiritually empty place are we trying to fill with constant affirmation, approval, and applause? The answers to these questions require consistent, intentional, disciplined spiritual work, and it is often helpful to make such a journey with a spiritual director or counselor or small group of trusted friends. Ultimately, we start with the recognition that our self-seeking behavior has spiritual roots, so inner work is not only helpful, it is necessary.

A second step is to be clear about who we are and who we are called to be. What are our gifts and graces? Not what gifts and graces do we wish we had, but what abilities and talents do we have now or could reasonably develop. Honesty, humility, and insight are required here. I have come to believe that our calling is best found at the intersection of our abilities and our opportunities. It is in that intersection that God is at work, long before we come to it. So, a solid step to avoid self-seeking behavior is to be clear about what we are called to do—our mission in life—and to be sure to join John the Baptist is affirming, *I am not the Messiah.* Surely our talents are needed in other intersections.

A third step to avoid self-seeking is to look for the unseen but needed tasks around your church. There are plenty of them: set up and clean up for activities, help with the landscape, work in the parking lot, purchase and make or bring the coffee, clean the coffee pots, volunteer in the office, restock the greeting material, organize storage areas, visit shut-ins, or give someone a ride to church or to the pharmacy. Of course, there are a multitude of other opportunities to serve. Look for them. The key is to intentionally be a part of the unseen army of volunteers that helps to make your church run smoothly. The rewards for doing so are intrinsic and eternal—a powerful antidote for self-seeking behavior.

Finally, if you recognize that you are someone who seeks the limelight or tries to save the circus, then take a break. Go on a vacation. Simply step back and let others step in. Honestly, it isn't always easy to do so, and it can be painful, but when we step back, we will see that others will step up, step in, and get the job done. Even though it may not be done exactly like we would have done it, the job will get done. Realizing that your church can and will go on without you is an important spiritual lesson for all of us to learn. As it turns out, perspective is everything.

Other Self-Seekers

Sadly, self-seekers seldom recognize that they are self-seekers. Somehow, such behavior brings on a sort of spiritual blindness, even though their incessant self-seeking is both obvious and irritating to others. Before I suggest some ways to deal gracefully with self-seekers in the church, I want to begin with a word of caution. If we find self-seeking persons especially irritating, it may be because they are a lot like us. So, before we launch a campaign to stamp down or stomp out self-seeking, a long and honest look in the spiritual mirror is in order.

Sometimes, starting a crusade against others can be an attempt to fill a spiritually empty place in our own lives. When his disciples asked Jesus why they couldn't cast out an impure spirit from a young boy, Jesus answered: "This kind can come out only by prayer" (Mark 9:29). Although casting out an impure spirit and dealing with an incessant self-seeker in your church are not exactly parallel events, I do believe that we can learn something from this passage, something that Jesus was trying to teach his followers—this kind can come out only by prayer. I take this to mean that when we step into the lives of others, we are to do so with a deep spiritual connection with the Father. We start and end with prayer, acknowledging that the Holy Spirit must do the heavy lifting. We are not the Messiah.

With that caution in mind, what steps can we take when self-seeking is running rampant in a messy situation? I will offer three. First, especially when individuals tend to run off and want to run the entire show, a good strategy is to organize teams to do the work rather than assign responsibility to any one individual. It will slow things down a bit and make the task more complex, but in this case, that's exactly what is needed to keep a self-seeker from running off in an ill-fated attempt to save the circus. Organize teams, carefully select leaders and conveners, and give each team a clear charge that outlines the intended scope of work. If the team strays (and some will), step in early and often to keep the team moving in the right direction and focused on the right things. Over time, solid teamwork is an effective way to mitigate self-seeking behavior, and teamwork is fun, too!

A second step is to organize a pathway for those who desire prominent leadership positions. I know of a church with a full music program. The minister of music constantly receives offers from those who want to sing or play a solo on Sunday morning or in the next big concert or holiday event. He always graciously and kindly thanks both parishioners and newcomers alike for their interest in helping out, and informs them that there is an established path of participation—soloists are selected from those who sing in one of the ensembles, and those who sing in the ensembles are selected from those who faithfully sing in the choir Sunday after Sunday. Likewise, instrumental soloists are selected from those who play each week in the orchestra. I think we can all learn from this approach. Before becoming the leader of the prayer team, it is fair to expect that one has been a faithful member of the prayer team. Before one is selected to be a small group leader, it is fair to expect that they have been an active and supportive member of a small group. Such an approach gives those who seek the limelight an understandable and expected path of participation to follow. You will find that some do; many do not. That's okay, too.

Finally, there are times when you have to kindly and gently say, "No, I'm sorry, but that won't work," or "Not now," or "Let's talk about how you can be involved here in some other way. We have so many needs." Of course, it is extremely difficult to be the gatekeeper, and it isn't much fun either. However, time after time I have seen the difficulties and messes that self-seekers make for congregations and ultimately for themselves, and it was because no one had the courage to say no and nip the dysfunction in the bud, even though it was clear that moving ahead would be a disaster. Saying no is difficult, but it is far better than having to live with the consequences of a poor decision. And remember, deciding not to make a decision and ignoring the consequences are decisions, too, and usually not good ones.

Conclusion

Self-seeking is a spiritual difficulty resulting in relational and organizational spillage. Dealing with self-seeking behavior in the church or in our own lives is a sticky wicket. It isn't easy to deal with incessant self-seekers we see around us or to even recognize, let alone deal honestly with our own tendency to seek the limelight, save the circus, or constantly seek validation from others. Yet, the Apostle Paul is clear: love is not self-seeking. It is no way to minister or serve others. Over time, self-seeking will torpedo any ministry—any ministry—draining the spirit of the organization and the energy of those who serve. And sadly, the organization (even a church) can lose its focus and lose its way.

When the church is in a mess, three forms of self-seeking tend to take root and grow: saving the circus, seeking the spotlight, and asking for validation—those who need constant affirmation, assurance, and approval. And to be honest, we can do it, too. So, what can be done to address these behaviors? As a start, it is important to recognize that they often are a result of a deep spiritual emptiness in one's life, and it cannot be ignored. In fact, it must be honestly and humbly addressed. Jesus' insistence is instructive here—we are the branches, not the vine, and to join John the Baptist in affirming, "I am not the Messiah." It is important to know who we are not, and to understand that our callings are found along other pathways, usually at the intersection of our opportunities and our abilities. And when we recognize these damaging activities in our own line of service, it is good to step back and take a break, letting others step up and step in. It is sometimes difficult but good to see that everything need not depend on us. In fact, it shouldn't.

When we must deal with self-seeking behavior in others, a good strategy is to organize efforts around teams rather than individuals, especially if persons are inclined to run off and leave everyone else behind. And it is also good to have a pathway to performance to demonstrate and insist that faithful service comes before the spotlight. It won't be popular with some, but it is ultimately helpful for everyone.

At the end of the day, I don't believe that there is any way to totally eliminate all modes of self-seeking behavior in church, or for that matter in our own lives. However, it can be recognized for what it is, dealt with intentionally and persistently, and channeled toward more healthy and helpful activities. Truly, love is not self-seeking, and self-seeking is no way to love, even when the church is in a mess—perhaps especially when it is in a mess.

Questions for Reflection and Discussion:

1. What type of self-seeker is most irritating to you: the circus saver, the spotlighter, or the validation seeker? Why?

2. What type of self-seeking have you experienced in church? What was the result?

3. Do you agree that self-seeking is ultimately a spiritual issue? Why or why not?

4. What type of self-seeking are you most tempted or inclined to engage in? What might you do to step back or step out in order to give others more space to serve and grow?

5. Why do you think self-seeking flourishes so easily in a messy church situation? What would be some pathways of performance that could mitigate these activities?

Love is patient, love is kind. It does not envy, it does not boast, it is not proud. It does not dishonor others, it is not self-seeking . . .

— 8 —

Love Is Not Easily Angered

> Anyone can become angry—that is easy, but to be angry with the right person and to the right degree and at the right time and for the right purpose, and in the right way—that is not within everybody's power and it is not easy.
>
> —Aristotle

Introduction

"In your anger do not sin," Paul wrote to the church in Ephesus, and went on to caution against letting the sun go down while we are still angry or giving the devil a foothold (Eph 4:26-27). We can take several things from this admonition. First, anger and sin are not siblings, but they are close cousins; they live in the same neighborhood. You can be angry and not sin, but it is easier to sin when you are. Second, since we can't do much to slow the setting of the sun, we must acknowledge and deal with our anger, and the sooner the better, preferably before we try to sleep. Finally, while Paul didn't come right out and say what kind of foothold the devil may gain from our anger, clearly any time we harbor anger and resentment, it is the soil in which all types of negative attitudes and actions flourish and take on a life of their own—certainly not the stuff of heaven.

So, how do we become angry, but with the right person, to the right degree, at the right time, with the right purpose, and in the right way? I think we can all agree with Aristotle—it is not easy, and Scripture from beginning to end is awash with stories about anger: some good, some bad, often ugly. In this chapter we will take an honest look at how to deal with anger in our own lives and what to do when it rears its ugly head in church. Sadly, if it isn't the result of a messy situation, it can certainly cause one.

Before we do, however, I want to share three examples of anger at work in a faith community, this time in a Christian university. I share these because I don't want to call out specific individuals who have behaved badly in church, but I could. In fact, we all could. Anger can plague the best of times in the best of places. Hopefully, we can draw some insight from these stories as we meditate on Paul's insistence that love "is not easily angered" (1 Cor 13:5b).

Easily Angered

Paul writes that love is not easily angered, and I think he's right, but we all know that anger can be easy, too. In the stories that follow, anger was misplaced, mistimed, and misused. I trust that we, all of us, will be able to connect the dots and see how such anger works against love at all turns.

Angry Parents

I was working at my desk on the second day of classes when an angry couple pushed their way past the office administrator and into my office, demanding that I immediately stop what I was doing and attend to their daughter's problem. It seems that she registered late for classes and was placed on the wait list for an elective class she wanted to take that semester. It was a very popular course, so there were others on the wait list as well. I tried to assure the parents that the dean was aware of the wait list and it would be addressed by the end of the day. That particular class didn't meet until Thursday, so there would be no loss of class time. "That's not good enough!" the mother yelled across my desk. "We won't put up with slovenly leadership. You're the provost and we pay tuition, so you work for us. If you are too lazy or too incompetent to do your job and fix this problem for our daughter immediately, we'll just have to go over your head to the president. I hope you lose your job over this!"

"The president's office is right next door," I told them as I escorted them out of my office and into the president's office. I looked at the president's executive assistant and said, "These parents demand to see the president, and I know he can receive them in about five minutes." The assistant gave me a funny look but slowly nodded her head in agreement. I returned to my office. Now, what the angry parents did not know was that the university president was called to a high church position the previous summer, so as provost I also served as acting president. And they also did not know that there was a way of getting into the president's office from a side door in my office. I quickly slipped out of my office, through the conference room, and into the side door of the president's office. In just a few minutes, there was a knock on the door and the angry parents stormed into the office. When they saw me sitting behind the president's desk, they stopped dead in their tracks, and when I said "Hello" with a welcoming smile on my face, the mother uttered a few choice words as they turned and marched back out the door.

That was the last time I saw the angry couple. I must be honest and admit that my first inclination was to make sure that their daughter did not get into that elective class as a way of punishing them for their nasty and entirely unnecessary anger—but I didn't. I checked with the dean and was told that the wait list had already been cleared and their daughter was in the class. As it turns out, their anger was totally unnecessary.

I have often wondered if they felt any remorse for their behavior, especially when their daughter called and told them that she was already in the class even before they arrived on campus. I guess I'll never know because I never heard from them again. As it turns out, anger often causes amnesia.

Angry at Church

I barely made it inside the entryway of the church when I was confronted by an angry father of a senior business student at the university. It seems that he and the faculty member who taught the senior seminar, the student's last class, had a major disagreement—the professor believed that the student had somehow cheated on the final exam and refused to submit a final grade until the matter was resolved, while the student adamantly held that the professor could not prove his accusations and demanded that the final course grade be posted immediately. Honestly, these situations are very difficult to discern. The wisdom of Solomon is needed, but he was nowhere to be found. As an experienced university administrator, I knew that there was a grade appeal process to be followed, and while it did not promise a quick resolution or that everyone would be satisfied in the end, it was as fair and objective a way to go as possible, stacking the decks neither in favor of the student nor the professor. Ultimately, if all else failed, I also knew that I would serve as the final arbitrator, but that was after all other measures of due process were concluded. Until then, my role was to see that the appeal went forward swiftly while remaining neutral.

The father didn't see it that way. In fact, he was angry, very angry. He wanted the grade posted and the professor fired, and he wanted me to see to it right then. I reminded him that we were standing in the church entryway on the Sabbath. I told him that I was not in a position to do anything in the next hour, or that day for that matter, since it was Sunday. The university was closed, I was in church to worship, and I would not pursue the topic with him, but I would be happy to meet with him and his son first thing in the morning in my office. This proved to be totally unsatisfactory. He followed me as I tried to walk away and cornered me once again in the back of the sanctuary. I asked him to stop as I tried to move away, but he pressed in and raised his voice even higher as he berated me for being an institutional lackey.

I managed to move away just as the service started, but as soon as the service was over, he pelted me once again with a barrage of disparaging accusations and demands for immediate action before I could even exit the pew. Finally, I told him in no uncertain terms that he had ruined my worship, and if he didn't step away immediately, I would call security. His behavior was embarrassing, ugly, and totally unnecessary. It was anger easily displayed at the wrong place, at the wrong time, to the wrong degree, and with the wrong person. Ironically, I waited for his call the following morning, having cleared my calendar so that I could meet with him at his convenience. He never called and he never came.

In the end, the appeal did go forward, bringing to light over the next week much more negative information about his son than the father knew or wanted to know. This, I've found, is often the case. It seems that students often "forget" to tell their parents all the facts, and with limited and sometimes entirely wrong information and faulty assumptions, anger comes too easily. Apologies seldom follow.

Angry Over Everything—and Nothing

In the first two stories, parents were quick to accuse and bully (anger in action), but slow to apologize or admit that they had acted inappropriately. Not so with Larry. He was a young faculty member with a brilliant mind, a large student following, and an outgoing personality, but he had a hair-trigger temper. As my dad would put it, he could get angry at the drop of a hat. Actually, he would get angry even when there was no hat to drop! He would take offense at an innocent comment someone would make in a faculty meeting, get angry while discussing the mission of the university at faculty lunch, attack a colleague after a committee meeting for their lack of agreement with him, or just lose it over some rumor about what the administration (that demonic entity on the other side of campus, or so he told his students) was planning to do without the consent of the faculty (or more precisely his consent). He had the facts wrong most of the time, but it never stopped him from throwing a fit, and he was good at it.

Like clockwork, later that day, Larry would go to the target of his anger (often me) and apologize for his behavior, weep and sigh uncontrollably, and ask for forgiveness. The first several times he did so, I was moved by his contrition and eager to reconcile and move on, but after a half-dozen or so episodes, it was clear to me that he was not only easily angered, he actually used his anger and apologies in a manipulative way as a form of power and control. Believing with Paul that love is not easily angered, I decided that I couldn't let his behavior continue unchallenged. It wasn't more than a day or two until he was back in my office, weeping and apologizing for an ugly display of anger after the faculty lecture earlier that afternoon. I told Larry that I did forgive him, but I didn't want any more apologies from him. He looked surprised. "No more apologies?" he asked. "That's right," I said, "I don't want you to come to my office, weep, and apologize because I want you to stop acting in such a way that you have to come to my office, weep, and apologize. Your apologies are a part of a very sad and sick circle of inappropriate behavior, and if you can't or won't control your temper, I will have to let you go. It's that simple. You can't teach here and continue to blow off and blow everything up." Now the tears erupted again in earnest as he confessed that his anger was his way of dealing with others and with his own insecurities. I suggested that it might be a symptom of something much deeper, something spiritual.

I am happy to report that he took my warning seriously, asked for help from several of his colleagues on campus who put him in touch with professionals who deal with anger issues (both emotional and spiritual), and his behavior and spirit improved. Every so often, Larry would drop by my office or see my on the campus mall. With a smile he would say, "Dr. Provost, you don't have to fire me this week!" and I would respond with a smile, "The week isn't over yet." We would both have a good laugh and be on our way. At the end of the day, love is not easily angered, and when it is, it is often an indication of much deeper issues.

The Anger Checklist

It doesn't take a rocket scientist to recognize the wisdom of Aristotle found in the epigraph at the beginning of this chapter, and it provides a helpful analytical tool for us when we find ourselves in an angry state of mind or spirit. I call it the Anger Checklist. It consists of a series of questions or queries that allow us to slow down, assess the situation, and avoid being easily angered or acting inappropriately when we are. Remember, anger in and of itself is not the issue. There are many good reasons to be angry. It's how we treat others and ourselves when we are, and what we are willing to do about our anger before the sun goes down.

Am I angry with the right person? Anger can easily be directed toward the wrong person. It is okay to become frustrated and perhaps even angry about a new or unjust store policy, but why take it out on the checkout clerk? They didn't make the decision, so direct your anger to those who made the decision, not an innocent bystander trying to get through the week. A bad day at work is not justification for kicking the dog when you get home.

Am I angry to the right degree? Anger can be metered out like a garden hose. When you are watering the plants, you don't just turn on the tap full bore. It will drown the plants, causing more harm than good. The same holds true for anger. With intention and care, you can meter out your anger, too. If your anger operates like a toggle switch (either all on or all off), there is some emotional and spiritual work to be done.

Am I angry at the right time? There is a right time (and place) to express your anger. Just before, during, and after church on Sundays isn't one of them, and public venues are best avoided, too. Anger expressed at the wrong time simply complicates an already troubled situation, doing more harm than intended good. Pick you battles.

Am I angry for the right purpose? What are you trying to accomplish by expressing your anger? Is it to right a wrong, defend a friend, or curtail abusive behavior—or is it to put someone "in their place" or "give them a piece of your mind"? Does it address or mitigate what caused your anger in the first place, or are you just wanting to get in the last word and feel better?

Am I angry in the right way? Anger can be constructive or destructive. Are you conducting yourself in a way that makes the situation better, or are your actions simply making things worse? For example, if you respond to the mistreatment of a coworker by spreading gossip all over the church, your anger may be justified but your response is clearly not.

If your answer is *No* or *I'm Not Sure* to any of the queries in the Anger Checklist, then stop, look, and listen. First, *stop*. I mean it. Just stop. Do it now! Don't do or say anything until you take an honest *look* at the entire situation: what just happened, why are you so angry, are there other feeling and issues coming to the surface, how are you dealing with your anger, what has happened as a result of your own actions? What part, if any, did you play in causing or complicating this situation? These questions are difficult and sometimes painful to address, but it is necessary to do so. Then, *listen*. Ask for help, seek counsel from a close friend or two, a counselor, or your mentor or spiritual director, and heed their advice. Let someone walk with you. And most importantly, take time to listen to the Holy Spirit who is always with you, especially in dire times, even angry times. Perspective, clarity, and courage are greatly needed in such times, and I know of no shortcuts for gaining them. Take time to stop, look, and listen. Misguided, misdirected, and misplaced anger only complicate matters, no matter how well-meaning you are or how just your cause.

And if we get to yes on the Anger Checklist, there's still some work to do. Anger is not simply, quickly, or easily dealt with. Thankfully, healing can come but I know of no instant cures. I will share several Next Steps right after we address one of the biggest anger issues I know—the idea of an angry God.

Scripture

You don't have to read Scripture widely or deeply to come across the understanding that God is angry, vengeful, and somewhat unpredictable. He is the supreme king who is easily angered. In the Old Testament stories, God's anger is seen in windstorms, hailstorms, volcanic eruptions, droughts, and floods, along with sicknesses, plagues, diseases of all sorts, and losing battles to invading armies—all evidences of God's retaliation for sin and unfaithfulness. Of course, they were trying to understand how God worked in their lives and in their faith communities, and it seems the best explanation they could come up with when bad things happened to them was that God was a very angry, jealous, and vengeful Actor, and their pain and losses were the result of someone's sin, probably their own. In a sad way, this is understandable. They were trying to make sense of the tragedies they experienced. Honestly, we do the same thing now, don't we?

And the flip side was also true. Their blessings—old age, abundant harvests, and large families—were the result of their faithfulness to God. So, if they were good, God blessed them, but if they were bad, watch out! And here's the rub, we carry the same spiritual DNA of that OT understanding of God with us today. A dear friend of mine was diagnosed with terminal brain cancer, and several Christians came to him and told him that his cancer was the result of some unconfessed sin. If he would only humble himself and confess his sins, God might still change his mind and spare his life. I have heard Christians explain the tragic loss of a son or daughter as God's way of trying to get their attention. I also know of Christians who earnestly believe that their new house is a gift directly from God for giving an extra ten percent in the offering plate on Sundays, and that tornadoes and floods in the Midwest are God's vengeance for an abortion clinic operating in Wichita.

Now, please hear me. I am not trying to make a political statement here, but I am saying that we carry poor (and I believe inappropriate) images of God, and these images color our lives of faith. Bad things do happen to good people and good things do happen to good people, and we, all of us, are trying our best to make some spiritual sense of it all—but we can't. The best I can do at times is to say that all of this is a mystery, and that life is messy but God is faithful. Beyond that, we are all walking along the road of faith in the dark, seeing and knowing only in part, to paraphrase the Apostle Paul (1 Cor 13: 9–12).

But if we agree with Paul that love is not easily angered, then it seems fair to conclude that God is not easily angered either, because God *is* love—a love that is patient and kind, always protecting, always trusting, always hoping, and always persevering (1 Cor 13:4, 7). That doesn't sound like an angry God to me, ready and eager to punish us at the drop of a hat, any hat. Pointing to an angry God is no way to justify our own anger. I truly believe that God doesn't work like that. We are much better served to embrace and model the images of God found in Psalm 23 (the good shepherd, the gentle guide, and the gracious host) or the loving and forgiving father in the story of the prodigal son (Luke 15:11–32). That's the God I have come to know.

Okay, I'll stop this sermonette. Rather than focusing our attention of God's anger, let's look at a few Next Steps in dealing with our own. As we all know, when church life gets messy, anger often plays a leading role.

Next Steps

Revisit the Anger Checklist

A painful fact is that we all justify our own anger. While it is easy to recognize that others may be operating with misplaced anger or misguided motives, our own anger always seems to be justified—to be normal. Many times, it is not. Very few of us can evaluate our own anger without bias, so that's where honest friends and good support come to the fore. Make sure your anger is within bounds.

Understand Anger's Impact

Sometimes anger can serve as a positive motivator, especially when facing injustice or trying to protect a colleague from organizational meanness, but that is the exception, not the rule. Anger by itself does not solve problems, and frequently makes things worse. It can hurt you, even make you sick. And anger is contagious, easily passed on like the flu, and when it fills the room, it clouds the issues and drives discourse underground or out to the parking lot.

Don't Be Afraid to Face Your Anger

Don't be afraid to face your anger. Often, we don't want to face these feelings because we know intuitively that where there is unprovoked and misplaced anger, there is pain there, too. Anger can be a manifestation of deeper issues such as insecurity and loneliness, and it can be a symptom of deeper spiritual issues. We start by summoning the courage to admit that we are angry, hold that anger closely, and then do some serious soul-searching and introspection. It is a journey better traveled with friends and support.

Focus Your Anger on Problems, Not People

It is far too easy to get mad at someone when it is really an organization problem, so it is best to focus your anger on the problems and policies rather than people immediately involved, particularly those who have little authority and played no part in developing the policy. Yelling angrily at a minimum wage gas station attendant or a hotel housekeeper may relieve some frustration, but it is unfair, uncalled for, and ultimately harmful to the attendant and to you. In addition, you look like a jerk. If you are rightfully upset, talk to the manager or their manager—or the owner. Focus on policy decisions and those who make them. Leave the others alone—for their sake, and for your own dignity.

Conclusion

Anyone can become angry—that's easy. It's how we use that anger and how we deal with it that makes all the difference. Are we angry with the right person, to the right degree, at the right time, for the right purpose, and in the right way? Honest answers to these queries will tell us if we are using our anger for good or for ill. And the Apostle Paul cautioned against holding on to our anger after sundown (Eph 4:26–27). I believe that he was saying to all of us that smoldering anger can hurt others deeply, and it always hurts us. Much better to step into action or step away than to carry anger around like a fragile egg. At the end of the day, lingering anger can make you sick—emotionally, physically, and spiritually.

Love is not easily angered. That's a powerful lesson for all of us, especially when our church life is in a mess and anger takes the leading role in the drama. We don't have to respond in kind. It may feel good at the time when we do, but it takes us and those around us down a very bad road. The key is to be angry and not sin, one of the narrowest roads we as Christians will ever be asked to walk—but walk we will. Thankfully, we never walk alone.

Questions for Reflection and Discussion:

1. On a scale of one (meaning not so good) to ten (meaning really solid), how would you rate your temper control? In other words, would you say that you are easily angered?
2. What types of things do you get angry about?
3. Which query on the Anger Checklist gives you the most pause? Why so?
4. Have you seen anger effectively managed in a church situation? Explain.
5. Have you seen anger usher in havoc and disarray in a faith community? Why was it so toxic?

Love is patient, love is kind. It does not envy, it does not boast, it is not proud. It does not dishonor others, it is not self-seeking, it is not easily angered . . .

9

Love Keeps No Record of Wrongs

"Love keeps no record of wrongs, but bitterness keeps detailed accounts."

—Craig Groeschel

Introduction

When we have been wronged, I'm not sure which process is harder: to let go and to move on or to forgive. To be sure, neither are easy, but both are necessary if we are to deal with the pain and hurt we carry with us, learn from them, and move on to better days. It isn't healthy to just ignore the wrongs that happen to us. Honestly, we can't for long, and we shouldn't. Selective amnesia is not the answer. Instead we must find ways to acknowledge and face our pain, and that takes time, but if we try to carry all of life's wrongs around with us like rocks in an old knapsack, they will weigh us down and become a bitter load. At the end of the day, they will wear you out.

And I am not sure how healing comes. Do we forgive in order to let go and move on, or do we let go and move on as part of the forgiveness process? Is it a series of identifiable steps or is it a process unique to each circumstance? In any case, if the key is to keep no record of wrongs, as Paul puts it, there must be a way forward. Thankfully, I believe there is, and I've come to believe that it is more of a process than a predetermined, sequential series of steps, perhaps more of a mystery. We'll look at this healing process, but before we do, I want to share a story about letting go and moving on. Hopefully, there will be a lesson in it for all of us.

The End of a Career in Ministry

Messy churches have a spotty history when it comes to personnel actions, and particularly so when it comes to letting people go or watching them leave. I think we hold churches to a higher moral standard because they do claim Christ, and I think we should, but time after time they fall far short of the mark, failing to treat employees and volunteers alike with grace and dignity when a change needs to be made or when the pastor decides to make a change. Whether they are dismissed or intentionally treated so miserably that they cannot in good conscience stay, it is truly a shame that so many dedicated church workers leave wounded, frustrated, and angry. And when a church is in a mess, it is easier for pastors to misuse their power in reckless and uncaring ways, mistreating and ignoring those who report to them. Sadly, more often than not, they do so with impunity—they are accountable to no one. Such was the case with Jonathan and his boss.

Jonathan was a career staff pastor, highly respected by the congregation, and a very kind man. He did his pastoral work with dignity and grace, and he was deeply loved by the volunteers who worked with him each week. Sadly, that may have been his downfall. The senior pastor decided that he no longer wanted Jonathan on his team, so he ramped up his criticism of Jonathan's work behind his back. He also stopped meeting with Jonathan for his semi-annual evaluations. In fact, he stopped meeting with Jonathan altogether. Still, Jonathan wrote to the senior pastor and made it clear that he had only two years left before retirement. He would do all he knew to do to make his last two years as productive and professional as humanly possible. He dearly wanted to end his career well and on good terms with his boss. At first the senior pastor agreed, but then suddenly changed his mind and forced Jonathan out by moving him to part-time, reducing his responsibilities, and having him report to another pastor who had previously reported to him. Under the circumstances, Jonathan was left with no choice but to resign. He did, and when he submitted his resignation, the senior pastor made it clear that there would be no going away celebration. All of this happened without any explanation. The senior pastor simply told the other staff members that Jonathan was no longer part of the team. He needed someone younger. It was a sad and sorry end to Jonathan's professional ministry at the church.

As you might expect, Jonathan was humiliated and deeply hurt. He wrote a note to the chairman of the board of trustees asking for an explanation and hoping for some type of intervention, but Jonathan was told in no uncertain terms that the board would not intervene. It was their job to support the senior pastor. In effect, the senior pastor could do whatever he wanted to do as long as he didn't run off with one of the office staff. Jonathan should just go away quietly and be thankful for the opportunity to work with such a gifted leader.

It was yet another slap in the face, and while it took some time for Jonathan to gather himself and regain his bearings, he did. He never lost his sense of humor or his generous spirit. He continued to serve faith-based community organizations and found several others that needed his expertise and valued his experience. He remained active in the community and became involved in several national ministry organizations. He golfed, biked, and skied with his friends, and spent time with his extended family. His self-confidence slowly returned. As a result, he was able to let go and move on. He told me that he had to come to terms with what happened to him. He still didn't like how he was treated, but he refused to let the actions of the pastor and the inaction of the board define him. They couldn't and wouldn't take away his spirit.

And when I asked him about forgiving the senior pastor, he smiled and said, "That's still a work in progress, but I am making my way. I think I'll get there, but I want it to be genuine, more than just saying the words. I want it to come from my heart." And if Jonathan has anything, it is a big heart. I think he'll get there.

Letting Go and Moving On

Jonathan's story is not a happy one. Mistreatment and hurt never are, but Jonathan found a way to summon something from deep within that gave him the courage to let go and move on. He found new avenues of ministry, too. Surely, it wasn't the way he wanted or planned for things to go, but they turned out to be real and rich, nonetheless. I think what he summoned from deep within was the love and grace of the Holy Spirit, who renews our spirits and calls us to holiness even after experiencing unholy treatment—even while experiencing unholy treatment. The pain and hurt do not disappear like playing cards in a magic trick, but over time they do subside, and new opportunities for service and ministry emerge. This is what happens when we keep no record of wrongs—when we let them go. It is the choice that confronts us all. We can either let go and move on, or we can sustain and carry a bitter account of the details. I don't think we have the emotional and spiritual bandwidth to do both. It is a choice with lasting consequences for us and for all of those around us. If love keeps no record of wrongs, then letting go and moving on are the loving things to do, and the person most loved in this scenario is you.

Sadly, some of us have a difficult time letting go, and some of us never do. I think of a young volunteer teacher in a primary Sunday school class in her local church. She was a well-known and highly respected public school teacher. The young and not so thoughtful senior pastor listened to her lesson from the hallway, and then walked into the classroom and corrected the teacher in front of her students. It was a trivial point, but his actions were not trivial. She felt that her professionalism as a teacher had been challenged, and she was so embarrassed that she walked away from church that day and never returned. That was more than forty years ago, and to this day attending any church is totally out of the question. The smoldering embers of that event long ago continue to give heat to her bitterness.

Without doubt, the pastor was totally wrong. Everyone deserves to be treated with respect, appreciated for their service. We all want to be seen and valued for what we do. That gives all of us a sense of dignity. But carrying a grudge from an embarrassment for forty years while withholding your gifts and graces is no way to live, even when the church is messy. The truth is that most churches are messy. So, how do we let go and move on?

I believe the keys to letting go are time, space, and perspective. First, letting go is a process, and processes take time. Rather than thinking of the letting go process in terms of days and weeks, think of it as a "letting go season." Other seasons will come, but this is your season right now, and seasons can't be rushed. It is a bit like wearing a cast for a broken arm. In a matter of days, we want it off, wondering why the arm is taking so long to heal. But as a mentor of mine once said to me about God's work in our lives, "When it seems like nothing is happening, something *is* happening." Letting go takes time, and just when we think we've let it all go, we run into someone or hear of an event and all the memories and emotions come flooding back. "Boy!" you say to yourself, "I thought I was over all of that, but I guess I'm not." The truth of the matter is that we may never be completely over all of that, whatever all of that is. Far better, I think, to work at letting go and moving on rather than trying to put a wrong behind you and act like it never happened. Letting go and getting over something are two different things. Focus on letting go and take your time.

It is also easier to let things go when we make some space for ourselves. Take a vacation. Take some time away. Stop following the events and activities of the church on social media or listening to the pastor's sermons online. Even meeting with a group of friends for dinner can keep the swirl of emotions going, and in a season of letting go, the last thing we need is more swirl.

One clarification is in order. Making space in our lives is not the same thing as going into hiding or staying at home with the blinds pulled. It is not healthy to act like a hermit but do be intentional and selective about what relationships you cultivate and sustain during a season of letting go. They are not all equally healthy and helpful.

Time and space are the requisite ingredients for prayer, contemplation, meditation, and reflection, and these are an essential part of the inner work that is needed to let go and move on. If we are going to keep no record of wrongs, which is to say that we aren't going to carry our hurts with us like a badge of honor, some serious questions must be examined. What just happened to me? What part did I play in the drama? Are there any apologies in order? What is God saying to me right now? Am I fixated on making a permanent record of the wrongs I experienced? How am I dealing with the bitterness? What can I learn from this season? Given my gifts and graces, what opportunities are open for me right now? What steps can I take to move on, even if they are just baby steps? When we honestly and prayerfully engage such questions, often with the assistance of a spiritual director or a close friend, we can gain a healthy perspective about what happened to us, who we are, and what we are called to do. Most importantly, we can see that God's mercies are new each morning—regardless of the season we are in.

Suffering wrongs is never easy, but they do come our way, even in church. We can't just get over them, and we shouldn't. They do change us, but they can change us for the better with time, space, and a healthy perspective. There is so much to be learned about ourselves, others, and God when rather than keeping a record of wrongs, we let go and move on—and we forgive, which may be the last thing we want to do and the hardest thing to do when we have been wronged.

Forgiving

To forgive does not mean that you approve of something or condone something or even like something. It is certainly more than just acting in a pleasant way, although even that can be helpful in certain uncomfortable social situations. Forgiving is deep, hard, honest, intentional spiritual work, and it demands the very best of us. Sometimes it demands more personal resources than we have to summon. That's okay, too, because forgiving is God's specialty. The Holy Spirit is the ever-present helper and teacher, and when we are wronged, we need all the help and wisdom we can get. Thankfully, they are freely offered to us and modeled for us.

To forgive can mean that you stop feeling anger toward someone or about something that has happened, or it can mean that you stop blaming someone for a wrong or stop blaming yourself for your part in the matter or simply for how you feel a week or two later. In the end, forgiving yourself may be the final stage in the forgiveness process. And I call it a process with good reason. We often think of forgiving as a single, final act that we do to put the entire wrong behind us and move on. Sometimes it does work that way, particularly if the other person is sincerely expressing remorse and seeking reconciliation, but not often. Viewing forgiveness as a process gives time for healing and hope. It is something that cannot be artificially rushed.

Perhaps the most profound way to understand forgiveness is to think of it as the cancellation of a debt—no repayment required, something no longer owed, not even an apology. Love keeps no record of wrongs, Paul tells us, meaning that that slate has been wiped clean. There are no accounts to be settled in court. The debt has been canceled, there is no basis for legal action. I admit that this is a hard teaching, but if we are to love in the midst of a messy church situation, this is exactly what is required of us if we are to experience reconciliation and renewal. And even if there is no interest in reconciliation and little prospect for renewal, we cancel the debt anyway. This allows us to let go and move on in due time, and more importantly, it allows us to act with spiritual integrity in the midst of anger, gossip, and confusion, and to accept the grace and healing that is offered to us by the Holy Spirit. It is ultimately a holy act.

In the end, forgiving is not easy, but it is an essential part of our spiritual growth and healing. Certainly, faith sends us on a spiritual journey and hope keeps us going, but it is love that bids us home. And love keeps no record of wrongs because if we do, we invite bitterness to be our traveling companion, and bitterness is simply a nasty, incompetent copilot. It has no interest in helping us through the messes we face or in finding our way home. Fortunately for all of us, that is another of God's specialties.

Scripture

"The war between the house of Saul and the house of David lasted a long time. David grew stronger and Saul grew weaker and weaker." So reports the writer of 2 Samuel (3:1). We can conclude three things from this short passage. First, they were at war and the war was nasty. The purpose of this war was to claim the throne and to consolidate military and political power. To do so, the opposition had to be wiped out, annihilated, thus ensuring that no one would step forward claiming to be the rightful heir to the throne, or make a military alliance with a another kingdom, or raise up an army from those who were displaced or disillusioned with the new king. This was all-out war.

Second, the war lasted a long time. What an interesting comment to be added to a story written so long ago. We can only imagine how terrible it must have been for ordinary citizens who were caught between these two warring factions, seeing their homes and shops and fields either confiscated or destroyed. And you can imagine the anger, contempt, and downright hatred that the armies had for each other. Long wars are especially unhappy wars, and this war lasted a long time.

Third, the house of David was winning and the house of Saul was losing. David's army had gained the upper hand and was pressing the battle, which spelled trouble for the house of Saul. Soon, the long war would be over, and the house of Saul would be only a memory. They would all be gone for good. And they were—except for Mephibosheth.

We'll get to him in a moment, but first let's be honest. There are parallels to be drawn from this short passage for a church in a mess. First, when church life is messy, it can feel a lot like war, and war is always nasty. We end up wondering why Christians would treat each other like they do, but sadly they do. Second, when the mess lasts a long time, everyone suffers. It drains the human spirit and any thought of good will is pushed away. And third, when it looks like others are winning and we are losing our standing and influence, we wonder if this spells the end—the end of our work, our influence, our best intentions, even our hopes and dreams. Simply put, when a church is in a mess, people get hurt—and the longer it lasts, the more the casualties, whether from frontal attack or friendly fire.

Back to Mephibosheth. After a string of victories, David claimed the crown over Israel and began to wonder if anyone from the house of Saul was still alive (2 Sam 9). He said that he wanted to show kindness as a tribute to his best friend, Jonathan, one of Saul's sons. Their friendship went back a long ways. David was told the one of Jonathan's sons was still alive. Mephibosheth was only five years old when Saul and Jonathan were killed, and when his nurse heard the news, she picked him up and fled. However, he was dropped, permanently injuring both feet. As a result, he was lame. In all likelihood, this saved his life since he was unable to later join in the fighting.

David had Mephibosheth brought to him, and I'm sure Mephibosheth thought that this would be the end of the road for him. His journey, however, was just starting. Instead of facing a death sentence, Mephibosheth was given all the lands that had belonged to his grandfather, King Saul. The income from these lands would provide a steady income for his family. What a turn of events! And that's not all. David instructed that he was to take all his meals at the king's table, to be treated like one of his own sons. When Mephibosheth came to David, he referred to himself as a dead dog, but he left feeling like one of the king's sons. It is a picture of grace and forgiveness and restoration all wrapped together—as it always is. Ultimately, it is because of the grace that has been extended to each of us that we are able to offer forgiveness to others. It is an expression of God's character, and forgiveness is an extension of God's grace.

Two final observations are in order. First, it is easy to think, "Oh sure, David kept no record of wrongs, but he was a king. He was special, an anointed one." Indeed, he might have been anointed for leadership, but he wasn't perfect by a long shot. Remember, shortly after the gracious story of David's restoration of Mephibosheth (2 Sam 9) comes the story of his affair with Bathsheba (2 Sam 11), truly one of David's low points. Clearly, *you don't have to be perfect to forgive*. David wasn't. None of us are.

The second observation is this: *forgiving doesn't make you perfect either*. Soon after David kept no record of wrongs when he dealt so graciously with Mephibosheth, he was the one asking God for forgiveness and restoration. Sometimes we are the one to offer grace and forgiveness—keeping no record of wrongs, and sometimes we are the one in need of grace and forgiveness, hoping that others will keep no record of wrongs. When we are challenged to love in such a way as to keep no record of wrongs, it is good to know that God operates in the same way with us. When we forgive, we are only modeling God's love and grace so freely given to us. Love keeps no record of wrongs, Paul writes. Deo Gratias!

Next Steps

If we are to keep no record of wrongs, particularly in a messy church situation, how do we go about such a daunting task? To be honest, there is no magic wand to wave to make the memories of the wrongs we suffer or the pain we feel simply disappear, but there are several steps we can take as we make our way toward healing and renewal, allowing us to let go, move on, and forgive in due time.

Lament

I was raised in the "keep your head up, have a stiff upper lip, put on a happy face, and please don't talk about your wounds" tradition. It has a long history. It demands that we swallow our pain, but when we do our stomachs keep score. Acting like our pain does not exist is no way to let go and move on. It simply doesn't work that way.

If we desire to keep no record of wrongs, the first step may seem counterintuitive: we acknowledge and embrace them. Remember what Jesus quoted from the cross: "My God, my God, why have you forsaken me?" (Ps 22:1). There was no mention of a good shepherd, a gentle guide, or a gracious host as celebrated in Psalm 23, even though I'm sure he knew that psalm well and believed in the goodness of his heavenly father. On the cross, he felt the pain of his wounds and wondered if God had forsaken him, and he said so. That's not a lack of faith. Rather, it's an honest expression of his faith in the face of pain, even death. We can and should do the same thing—lament. Let God know how we feel, even if how we feel is mad as hell. God can take it. In fact, I believe that God invites us to come as we are. It's the first step in keeping no record of wrongs.

Go at Your Own Pace

Healing takes time—and it has to be your time. Don't try to rush through the process as if it were some type of board game. Take your time. Be comfortable with the pace of your recovery. God is. And even if your best friends get impatient and urge you to hurry up and "get over it," whatever "it" is, don't. You can't heal according to their wishes. Don't let others push for an instant recovery. It doesn't work like that. Go at your pace.

Do the Inner Work

There is a big difference between going at your own pace and simply being stuck in the mud. If we are to keep no record of wrongs, there is honest and earnest inner work to do—prayer, meditation, contemplation, reflection, examination, and analysis. After, and even as we lament, we ask the Holy Spirit to speak to us and work on us, providing illumination, inspiration, courage, and grace as we face our wounds and begin to summon the strength to let go and move on.

But doing inner work does not necessarily mean solo work, although there is much good in private prayer and meditation. Often, a spiritual advisor, counselor, or mentor can be of great assistance as we embrace the pain we feel, work to make some sense of what we have experienced, and think about how to move on with courage and grace.

Focus Forward

If we desire to let go and move on, keeping no record of wrongs, at some point we have to begin looking forward to what might be next rather than simply holding and examining our wounds. To be sure, lament is necessary, and going at our own pace and doing the inner work are necessary, but what might be next? What are our gifts, graces, and opportunities? I have come to believe that God's will for our lives is best found at the intersection of our abilities and our opportunities. Look for them. Take a humble step.

Forgive as You Can

If the ultimate goal is to extend the same grace and forgiveness to others that God has extended to us, let's be honest and admit that it isn't always easy, especially to those who have betrayed our trust, hurt us deeply, or quashed our hopes and dreams. After all, we're not God, but we are called to be holy, and forgiving is holy business. I do believe that if we are sincere about keeping no record of wrongs, it means that we must let go, move on, *and* forgive—in due time. It can't be rushed, it must be heartfelt, and it often takes more resources than we think we have. Let God do the heavy lifting, working for us and through us and in us. Forgiving someone may change the dynamics of the situation, but even if it doesn't, it will certainly change us. We are shaped and formed far more from the valleys of our lives than by our mountain top experiences.

Lament, go at your own pace, do the inner work, focus forward, and forgive as you can. It is an uninvited journey, but a formative one if we desire it to be so.

Conclusion

When the Apostle Paul wrote to the church in Corinth, a church in a big mess, and told them that love keeps no record of wrongs, I doubt that it was received with great joy. Think about it. When we have been wronged, our first instinct is not to let go, move on, and forgive. That sounds too much like giving up without a fight, and when we are wounded, we do want a fight, a pound of flesh, an eye for an eye. We want others to pay for their actions and feel the pain we now feel. We want justice. This is totally understandable.

I am guessing that the Corinthians felt the same way. After all, if you keep no record of wrongs, how are you going to go to court, sue for damages and prove your case, or convince the church that you have been mistreated? You *have* to keep a detailed record of wrongs to order to win in the legal courts or in the court of public opinion.

Yet Paul insists that there is a better way. Love is patient and kind, and among other things, it keeps no record of wrongs. Honestly, I don't think we can do this by ourselves, and thankfully, we don't have to. We have the gift of the Holy Spirit, the ever-present teacher, who works in us and through us, giving us courage, shaping us, and calling us to a holy life. We simply do our best to model the grace that has been extended to each of us. That we can do. Even though the path to forgiveness will take us on a long journey, love will bring us home. That's a promise.

Questions for Reflection and Discussion:

1. When you have been wronged, what is the hardest thing about letting it go? Is it pride, anger, the desire for justice, or something else? Explain.
2. Have you ever had difficulty moving on from a hurtful incident? What held you back, how did you move on, and what strategies would you suggest for someone in that situation?
3. Do you think that it is possible to forgive someone who is unapologetic and unconcerned about the pain they have caused, particularly when they are not held responsible for their actions? Why or why not?
4. What is the best way for you to do "inner work"? Are you more comfortable working by yourself or in the company of others? Which way is more effective for you? Why?
5. Why do you think so many leave church work wounded? Can you think of someone who let go, moved on, and forgave in the midst of a messy church situation? What was the result?

Love is patient, love is kind. It does not envy, it does not boast, it is not proud. It does not dishonor others, it is not self-seeking, it is not easily angered, it keeps no record of wrongs. . . .

— 10 —

Love Does Not Delight in Evil

The world is a dangerous place to live; not because of the people who are evil, but because of the people who don't do anything about it.

—Albert Einstein

Introduction

This is the end of Part II, Love Out of Bounds, a string of eight emotionally and spiritually tough chapters, tough on the reader and tough on the writer, too—envy, pride, boasting, self-seeking, dishonoring others, anger, keeping records of wrongs, and now refraining from delighting in evil. To be honest, I look forward to Part III, discussing the kind of love that always rejoices, protects, trusts, hopes, and perseveres. That will be much more fun to write about, much more uplifting. But before we move on, it is important to spend some time looking at this one last behavior that pushes the boundaries of love, and pushes our buttons, too.

Love does not delight in evil, the Apostle Paul writes with good reason. When the church is in a mess or we're in the middle of a mess or both, it is far too easy to delight in others' failures or condone behaviors and activities that would otherwise be clearly out of bounds. And we all know of many evil acts over the centuries that have drawn from and been carried out with deep religious conviction, often in the name of Truth or God. While it would be interesting and instructive to look at some of these evil acts done in God's name, let's stay a bit closer to home, looking instead at how we overlook and excuse negative behaviors in our churches and in our own messy lives, and why it is so tempting and self-satisfying to gloat over the failures of others. This we will do, but first a story.

It Grew Back

The news came to us through the prayer chain at our local church. I've always felt that there was a very fine line between prayer chains and just plain gossip, but this message was in earnest. We were asked to pray for a pastor in town who was on leave, experiencing physical difficulties, and requesting our prayers, so pray we did. We prayed for him each morning at home, and at church at midweek prayer meetings and during Sunday morning services. After a month or so, we were informed that prayers of a different kind were in order. The pastor was now living in Lansing with his new girlfriend, having left behind his wife and three young children. In such a small community, the news was stunning.

As it turned out, a good deal of prayer was in order. When several concerned parishioners first confronted the pastor about rumors of his affair, he vehemently denied the rumors and the church board stood with him, even asking his accusers to leave the church if they couldn't support the pastor. And after details began to emerge, the board first blamed others for not protecting the pastor, then for taking advantage of him, and finally for not forgiving the pastor for his wayward ways. As all this played out, they created an alternative explanation for his absence—that he was sick and in need of some time off. Finally, when the board came clean, reporting accurately but vaguely about what had happened, the pastor was gone but the mess remained. Now our prayer chain kicked in again, this time praying for the search for a new pastor. Oddly enough, we were never asked to pray for the pastor or his wife and children as they looked for a new home, something that our family did anyway at the insistence of our mother. She always championed the underdog, the down and out, and those of the margins of either community or church.

I was probably twelve at the time, so I was not theologically sophisticated, but even at that age, things didn't quite add up. Why did we pray for the pastor's health problems when he wasn't sick at all? Why did the trustees send out a false prayer request? And why did the pastor leave his wife and children? According to our theology, we all needed to be forgiven for our sins (to be saved) and we all needed to have the carnal root removed (to be sanctified—to eradicate "our bent toward sinning"). I remember many prayer meeting testimonies about being saved *and* sanctified, with all temptations, cravings, and worries gone for good. It was all peace and joy. But how then, I wondered, could the pastor with his carnal root removed sin by leaving his wife and children and running off with someone else? It didn't make any sense. When I asked my mother about the pastor's carnal root, she looked and me and said, "It must have grown back." I didn't know what to say then—and I still don't.

But I do know that when we are confronted with nasty stuff—evil in a variety of forms—it is tempting to overlook, hide, excuse, blame, justify, and even modify our theology to make things fit. Yet Paul is quite clear: love does not delight in evil. He is right, of course, and we'll look at two all-too-common ways that we delight in evil—condoning and gloating. This is going to come very close to home for most of us.

Condoning

Tolerance is a virtue, at least most of the time, but certainly not in this case, not when it comes to evil. When Paul writes that love does not delight in evil, we eagerly agree. "Of course, love doesn't! We would never think of doing that kind of thing." However, the kind of thing that we are thinking about is the picture of an ISIS fighter lifting his weapon and rejoicing at a suicide bomber's slaughter of an innocent wedding party. Of course, we wouldn't do that! We don't rejoice in *that* kind of evil.

But there are subtler forms of evil and ways of delighting that come much closer to home. What if we substituted the word condone for delight? Paul's admonition would read something this way—love does not *condone* evil. That, I have seen far too many times in communities that claim Christ. I have seen nasty and sinful acts simply ignored or overlooked for the sake of the reputation of the church and the leader. I have witnessed the shooting of the messenger, and the truth of the message hidden, justified, and excused. And I have seen the innocent bear the brunt of blame, criticism, and shunning for bringing up the matter in the first place, even though they were the victim, not the perpetrator or predator.

Honestly, I didn't always know how to respond at the time, and I still have difficulty in knowing what to say about it or how to explain why this happens, but I know that it has happened, and it continues to happen today. Why? I think that there are three forces at play. First, churches operate with an air of trust. Thus, church leaders at all levels have a great deal of authority and power, but very limited accountability, if any at all. Put another way, churches lack the control structures and mechanisms common to most other organizations. They don't trust but verify; they simply trust. As such, leaders can do just about anything they want without scrutiny, and sadly, what they do is not always good for themselves or the church they are called to serve. The church ends up serving the leader. This flip-flop is all too common, but never healthy.

Second, when someone comes forward with troubling accusations that are vigorously denied, it is often difficult to determine who is telling the truth. The default is to believe the leader, especially when there is "pastor worship" in play, a condition where the pastor or leader has been placed on a pedestal, admired, and followed as if they can do no wrong, even when they do. So, the messenger is shot. They are accused, excluded, and blamed for the message. Of course, there should be a presumption of innocence until proven guilty, but pastor worship prevents even the thought of a fair hearing into the facts of the matter. Presumed innocent until proven guilty becomes simply innocent. No questions asked, and no need to investigate.

Third, those who are vested with the organizational obligation to oversee and investigate accusations of wrongdoing are insiders. That is, they have been invited into positions of lay leadership and carry an enormous personal commitment to the church and to the leader. So much so that the idea of bad press or embarrassment that would damage the image and programs of the church are unthinkable. The default is to try to minimize or justify the actions of the leader and make the complainant go away—silently, unnoticed, and unheard—for the sake of the organization. It usually takes the courage and persistence of a few who will stand in opposition and not let the issue be buried, and it often comes at an enormous personal cost for those who do. Sadly, it is often those who stand for the truth who are marginalized and labeled as troublemakers.

As you can see, when we seek to overlook, justify, or hide wrongdoing for the sake of the church, it is the integrity of the church that is ultimately damaged. Truly, love does not delight in evil, and there is an enormous price to be paid when we do, no matter how well-intentioned our actions. It is love misplaced and clearly out of bounds.

Gloating

I don't think we often associate gloating with delighting in evil, but I think we should. To gloat is to feel and show excessive satisfaction with your own success or with the misfortune of another. Have you ever heard someone say, "What goes around, comes around. I hope they get what they deserve, and when they do . . ."? Maybe you've even said it yourself. I have. And when someone falls or fails, how do you receive the news? I must confess that I've laughed out loud and did the happy dance on more than one occasion. The news made me feel better, justified and satisfied in some strange way. However, Paul insists that when we gleefully or smugly, even maliciously, take pleasure in someone's failings, we are over the line and out of bounds. Love doesn't go there, even when the church is in a mess.

Why? What is wrong with a little self-righteous gloating? The answer, in many ways, is self-evident. It is precisely because it is self-righteous, having pride accompanied by a sense of moral superiority. That always spells trouble. Gloating over the failings of another is no way to feel better about ourselves. Our identity is in Christ. We are not defined by our failures or the failures of others, even those who have hurt us. Delighting in others' misfortunes takes us on the low road straight into the mess.

And even when someone "gets what they deserve," it is rarely an isolated event. There are always innocent victims who are hurt and must try to pick up the shattered pieces of their lives—a spouse, children, family, close friends, co-workers, other leaders, a congregation, even a community. When we gloat, we can get so caught up in our own celebration that we fail to remember those who face a painful and uncertain future. Love does not delight in evil; it neither condones misbehavior nor gloats at the failings of others. When the church is in a mess, both are tempting but clearly out of bounds.

The love that Paul writes about is a forgiving love, a tough love, particularly tough on us. It does not permit or excuse self-serving, self-seeking, or self-righteous behavior. Rather, it is a love that calls us to protect, to trust, to hope, and to persevere—all the time, always. This is the high road that keeps us above the mess, even though we feel overwhelmed by the mess. In the next chapter, we'll move from delighting in evil to rejoicing in the truth. It is a worthy destination.

Scripture

I want us to look at two stories from the Old Testament. To be clear, these stories were not written about us, to us, or for us, but there is still much wisdom to be drawn from them, offering instruction and guidance as we navigate our way through the messes we face in church and at home—without delighting in evil. It isn't always easy, but it is the right thing to do.

Eli and His Sons: 1 Samuel 2:13 and 3:4–18

Eli was the high priest in Shiloh who was entrusted with the upbringing and mentoring of a young boy named Samuel. This he did extremely well. Samuel became one of the most important and influential figures in Israel's history, but he didn't do so well with his own family. According to 1 Samuel, "Eli's sons were scoundrels; they had no regard for the Lord" (2:13). They bullied worshipers in order to get the very best cuts of meat that were brought for sacrifice, and they took advantage of the women who served at the entrance to the tent of meeting. This Eli knew, first by rumor, then by a prophetic warning from "a man of God" who came to Shiloh for that very purpose, and finally by a direct warning from God delivered by the young Samuel.

Still, he did nothing about it other than to express his concern about the way they were acting, even though he had the power and authority to put a stop to it. And even though Eli clearly understood that God was displeased with his inaction, he simply shrugged his shoulders and said that God would do what God would do (1 Sam 2:3). Eli continued to condone, ignore, and overlook their evil acts for decades, and he paid a high price for it. Love does not delight in evil.

The Edomites: Obadiah 1:11–12

The Edomites were Judah's neighbors. They weren't the best neighbors in the world, but neighbors, nonetheless. When Jerusalem was attacked and overrun by the Babylonians, they remained aloof (Obad 1:11). They stood by and watched their neighbor's misfortune. They could have come to their aid, but they didn't. And to add insult to injury, they rejoiced and gloated at their defeat and humiliation (1:12). They enjoyed it. They celebrated it.

All of this was too much for Obadiah, who through a vision from God took the Edomites to task, calling them out for not coming to the aid of their neighbor and then for gloating about it. It was a clear case of delighting in evil. God didn't like it a bit, and through Obadiah, said so in no uncertain terms. Obadiah is the shortest book in the Bible. God didn't mince any words.

* * *

There is much for us to take from these two stories. In the case of Eli, he stood by and watched his own family, his sons, disgrace the temple and disrespect and dishonor the women who worked there, even though he could have stopped it. He had the power to do so, and he had the moral responsibility to do so, but he didn't do anything. That was wrong. Love does not overlook evil.

And the Edomites did not lift a finger to help their neighbors in their time of desperate need, and then gloated about their downfall afterward. God, through the prophet Obadiah, made it clear that love does not behave that way either. It does not delight in evil; it does not stand idly by nor gloat over the misfortune of neighbors. Our families and our neighbors deserve better. Love demands it, calling us to a higher standard. Paul tells us that love does not delight in evil. He is right in doing so.

Next Steps

If we are not to delight (or overlook or condone or gloat) in evil, what can we do to keep this temptation at bay? Let me offer five action steps.

Accountability Policies and Structures

First, in churches (and in all organizations) it is important to build accountability policies and structures into everyday operations, especially when it is in a mess. No one should have unrestricted and unsupervised access to organizational funds or unfettered treatment of people. When they do, bad things tend to happen. This does not mean that we don't trust people. We do, but remember, the church is a human organization with a heavenly mission. Bad things can happen, we know that, so accountability is a form of protection from unfair accusations and from our own temptations and poor judgement. If we know that bad things can happen when no one is looking, we need to make sure that someone is looking.

No Pastor Worship

Second, I believe that we are called to love, support, and encourage our pastors, but not to worship them. When we put our leaders on a pedestal, we engage in pastor worship and it is easy to forget that they are just like us. They are human. They can make mistakes, and they can cross the line from time to time. And if they do, pastor worship makes it difficult, sometimes even impossible, to hear and respond to an accusation of wrongdoing because we believe that the person we worship can do no wrong. If we are not to delight in evil, it is good to love, support, and encourage our pastors, but reserve our worship for God.

Take Accusations Seriously

We shouldn't believe everything we hear, of course, but we should take accusations of misconduct seriously. It is important to refrain from shooting the messenger, no matter how troubling their accusations are or how much trouble their accusations may cause the church. And it is important to spell out clear policies and procedures in writing about how accusations of misconduct will to be handled *before* they are needed. And the same holds true for employee grievance procedures. Spelling them out in advance can save a good deal of time, frustration, and embarrassment, not to mention a lawsuit or two.

Don't Gloat—Reach Out

When someone "gets what they deserve" or "what's coming to them," the temptation is to do just a bit of gloating, at least in private. I get that, but I doubt that gloating at someone's misfortune is a mature Christian response, particularly since we are instructed to love our neighbors as ourselves (Matt 22:36-40; Mark 12:28-31; and Luke 10:27). I think that includes their families, too. Better to remember that others are hurt when someone fails, and to make a concerted effort to reach out to them in some meaningful way if we can. And if we can't, at least to be mindful of them and remember them in our prayers. This is not a spiritual bromide; it is a faithful act of joining with the Holy Spirit to bring hope and healing to those who suddenly find themselves in the desert. We've all been there at one time or another.

Reflect and Go Deeper

Finally, whether you experience or observe or just hear about someone's misfortune in a messy church situation, it is good to take some time to reflect on the event, and to think seriously and deeply about what you might learn and how you might grow from the experience. What might God be teaching you in this moment? Take time to reflect and go deep. It may be the best way to avoid delighting in evil. It is certainly a good way to deepen your own spiritual journey.

Conclusion

When the church is in a mess, it is easy to delight in evil. Of course, we do not delight in obvious forms of evil—terrorism, sexual abuse, mass shootings, and the like—but we can and do engage in subtler forms of evil when we ignore, overlook, or cover up wrongdoings in our midst or gloat at a neighbor's misfortune when we could have stepped in and helped out. From Scripture, it is clear that God does not approve of such actions, nor should we.

Church life is messy for most of us, and for all of us at one time or another. Better to anticipate difficulties in advance and establish thoughtful policies and procedures to deal with allegations of misconduct rather than to live in denial that such things can happen in our church. When we do, the first response is often to shoot the messenger, and from there, things tend to go from bad to worse for everyone. We can and must do better; love demands it. Love does not delight in any form of evil.

* * *

In Part II, we have examined a litany of behaviors and attitudes that drive love out of bounds. Delighting in evil is the last one on the list, and perhaps the most destructive, at least in part because it is so subtle—hard to recognize, hard to admit, and even harder to deal with. Thankfully, Paul does not leave us in despair, but offers us a glimpse of love "at its best," a love that rejoices in the truth, and always protects, always trusts, always hopes, always perseveres. When our church is in a mess, "always" is the glue that holds things together, holds us together. We'll celebrate these aspects of love in Part III.

Questions for Reflection and Discussion:

1. Have you ever witnessed or been involved in a case where a difficult or embarrassing allegation about the church or its leadership was simply overlooked, swept under the rug, or rationalized away? What was the end result?

2. Why is the messenger so often blamed for the difficulty they speak about as if they were the troublemaker? What is at work in these situations?

3. Why is it so easy for us to gloat at another's failure? Do you think it is simply a human reaction or are there spiritual implications for us when we do?

4. There is the fine line between supporting your pastor and pastor worship. Do you agree that pastor worship is unhealthy? Why or why not?

5. Regarding your own spiritual journey, what aspect or idea from this chapter challenged you most? Why?

*Love is patient, love is kind. It does not envy, it does not boast,
it is not proud. It does not dishonor others, it is not self-seeking,
it is not easily angered, it keeps no record of wrongs.
Love does not delight in evil . . .*

PART III

Love At Its Best

When a church is in a mess, it requires patience and kindness of immense proportions, spiritual proportions. And when it is our own church, it requires that of each of us. When we are caught up in the mess, we yearn for a love that delights with the truth and always protects, trusts, hopes, and perseveres. That is love at its best when it is needed the most.

According to the Apostle Paul, love can be expressed in these terms. That is to say, we can live this way. It isn't always easy, and it may seem to others to be a bit silly, but it is love at its very best. It is a love that overcomes in the most difficult situations and in our darkest moments. In part III, we will look with confidence and hope at five aspects of love that can carry us through terrible times. If faith sets us on a spiritual journey and hope keeps us going, it is love that bids us home. Such a journey requires love at its very best.

11

Love Rejoices With The Truth

> The Word became flesh and made his dwelling among us. We have seen his glory, the glory of the one and only Son, who came from the Father, full of grace and truth.
>
> —JOHN 1:14

Introduction

LET'S FACE IT. THE truth isn't what it used to be. I recently heard a lawyer representing a major political figure defend the fact that this figure had not told the truth on numerous occasions, most of the time, in fact, which is another way of saying that he lied on a regular basis. The lawyer said, "Well, he wasn't under oath." Not under oath? That struck me as a legal response, not a moral answer, not a spiritual answer. Are we only obligated to speak the truth when we are in a courtroom with one hand raised in the air and the other hand on a Bible? And when the church is in a mess, do we have the clearance to say what we want about who we want to help the church avoid embarrassment or encourage someone to move on? I don't think so. We who claim Christ are called to a higher standard than that. We don't tell the truth because we are under oath. We tell the truth because Christ became flesh and made his dwelling among us and lived here on earth *full of grace and truth*, as John puts it (1:14). Full of truth. I take that to mean all the time.

Of course, I have lived long enough to know that when we start a discussion about truth, it can go south quickly, and particularly so when we are speaking about what some refer to as biblical truth. That is, the truth we glean from the Bible. I was taught from an early age that the Bible contains truth. No, it is *the* truth. It is God's word to all of us. We read it and there it is, much like the words that Moses brought down from Mt.

Sinai to the children of Israel on stone tablets. It was to be received and obeyed. End of discussion.

However, after some years of earnestly living out the call of Christ and working with some very good theologians, I have come to believe that it isn't quite that simple. With theologians, few things are. For me, the pursuit of truth is an eternal conversation, and a complex one, too. It requires humility, hospitality, insight, and courage. In this chapter, we are looking at the second half of 1 Corinthians 13:6: "Love . . . rejoices with the truth." Rejoices *with* the truth. That's interesting. Some versions, the King James Version among them, use "in" instead of "with." Love . . . rejoices *in* the truth. Rejoicing *in* the truth gives me the impression that truth is static, cast in stone, while rejoicing *with* the truth conveys a sense of embrace. We embrace truth and celebrate it.

And the expression I like best is found in The Message Bible: Love "takes pleasure in the *flowering* of truth" (1 Cor 13:6b). For me, the flowering, the unfolding of truth, captures the actual nature of truth. It grows on us. As even the Apostle Paul clearly writes, "For now we see only a reflection as in a mirror; then we shall see face to face. Now I know in part; then I shall know fully, even as I am fully known" (1 Cor 13:12). Simply put, he admitted that he didn't know everything. Neither do we.

At the same time, Paul admitted that he did see, if only a reflection; and he did know, if only in part. So when we speak about truth, even biblical truth, perhaps especially biblical truth, we must do so with both confidence and humility. We have confidence in what we see and know, but we must have the humility to admit that we don't see or know everything. We could be wrong. Truth isn't a stone tablet, but rather a flowering plant—both firmly planted but tender and growing. That's why many believe that the truth of things is best explored and explained in a community of faith where hospitality is shown for different points of view, different interpretations, different contexts, and different readings of sacred texts. The pursuit of truth becomes an honest and earnest conversation where power and egos are left at the door, space is given for other points of view, and learning and growing are more important than being right. Sadly, such hospitality seems to disappear when the church is in a mess

Late in his ministry, Jesus told his disciples: "when he, the Spirit of truth, comes, he will guide you into all the truth" (John 16:13a). The Spirit will guide you into all the truth. *Guide you. Into.* These are not cast-in-stone words. These are not "we know the truth and everyone else is wrong" words. Rather, they imply movement, maturation, a flowering and growth in understanding. As it turns out, truth is more than it used to be. It continues to flower before us, with us, and within us, too.

How the Truth Has Flowered for Me

When I look back, I can see that I had a few firmly developed ideas about God and what constituted the spiritual life, a holy life, when I left for college. They were not fully developed, but they were the truth as I understood it. My theology wasn't deep, but what I believed, I believed adamantly. Over the years, however, while some of my assumptions about God and holy living have been affirmed, others have changed. The truth has flowered for me, and for that, I give thanks. The foundation of my faith is still firm, but my theology has a few more windows and a few less walls, many more questions and a few less answers. For that, I am thankful, too.

What follows are some examples where my spiritual assumptions have flowered. The list is personal, and it is not exhaustive. Your list will be different. That's perfectly okay. It should be. However, if your assumptions about God, worship, and spiritual growth have not changed in any way over the years, I challenge you to revisit your assumptions. If the Spirit is to lead us into all the truth, as Jesus said, then we are called to journey, to be led. We don't stand still. Rather, we follow the guidance of the ever-present teacher.

What You Don't Do Makes You Holy

I grew up in a small church, a holiness church as we would describe ourselves. There was an emphasis on getting saved, to be sure, and an even greater emphasis on being sanctified. That required a second work of grace, represented by a second trip to the altar. After that, it was all about living a holy life, but even at a young age it struck me that it was more about not doing anything fun than about living abundantly. That is, there was a long list of things that we holiness people didn't do, and that made us holy: no drinking, no smoking, no crude language, no shorts, no makeup, no earrings, no sports, television, or eating out on Sundays, no movies, no dancing, no circuses, and no to just about anything else that seemed to me to be any fun at all. To be holy, I learned, was defined and determined by what we didn't do, and there was a lot we didn't do!

When I left home for college and beyond, it became clear to me that this way of being holy didn't make much sense, and some of the restrictions were just plain silly. As a result, many of my contemporaries rejected church and Christianity altogether because they lacked any way of expressing what holy living looked like. They had only been told how not to live, but not how to live out the love of Christ in any meaningful way. This was, and is, very sad.

Over the years, my understanding of holiness has flowered. It has grown away from a long list of pious restrictions and toward an understanding that the call to holiness is real, but the intent is to become like Christ, to love God with everything we have and to love our neighbors as if our very lives depended on it. I believe they do. This is my understanding of the call to holiness that has flowered over the years and motivates me yet today.

You Have to Empty Yourself to Be Spiritual

Along with the idea that holiness was a long list of "don't do this and don't do that," I also came to believe that the way to be holy was to totally empty myself and let Christ inhabit my body, my mind, my very being. I think it started when visiting missionaries testified that they had dreamed of being a doctor, but God sent them to the mission field instead. All thoughts of what we might want to do or be were simply off limits. Our job was to become empty vessels through which God could work, and I worked at it as best I could, but honestly I fell short so many times that I constantly felt like a spiritual failure and a holy fraud.

I'm not sure when or how it happened, but somehow I came to the realization that God did not want me to be empty, to be a spiritual zombie, just a shell of a person waiting to be taken over by the Spirit. Instead, God wants me to be full—full of hope, full of dreams, full of passion, full of talent, full of grace, full of courage, full of love. These are the things that God uses to accomplish his purposes. Just as my understanding of holiness has flowered, so has my sense of the part I play in ministry to others.

Success Equals God's Blessing; Sickness or Disaster Equals God's Punishment

During my high school years, I believed that God and I had struck a good deal. If I was good—honest, sincere, and pious, God would bless me with a college scholarship, a good-looking girlfriend, popularity, and maybe even a new car. All these things were the fruits of a faithful Christian life. On the other hand, if things didn't pan out, it was the result of some unconfessed sin on my part or on the part of someone close to me. God blessed those who honored him and punished those who didn't. It was that simple, and easy to find evidence of this arrangement in the Old Testament. It seemed that God was a demanding taskmaster and a broker of rewards and punishments.

Then I began to think seriously about the words of Jesus reported in Matthew's gospel: "He causes his sun to rise on the evil and the good, and sends rain on the righteous and the unrighteous" (5:45b). This didn't seem like much of a bargain to me—and it wasn't. I saw that God is not in the business of blessing every good person (hopefully me) and punishing every bad person (hopefully someone else). It also became clear to me that claiming Christ was not an insurance policy against bad things happening to us. It didn't remove us from the human race.

My theology has been boiled down to this: *Life is messy.* It either is, has been, or will be. That's life. You can count on it. But you can also count on something else: *God is faithful.* "His love endures forever" (Psalm 136:2b); his compassions "are new each morning, great is his faithfulness" (Lam 3:23); "As the mountains surround Jerusalem, so the lord surrounds his people both now and forevermore" (Psalm 125:2). That's not just a good bargain for me. That's a wonderful promise for all of us. Thanks be to God!

God Has a Perfect Plan for Your Life and You Have to be Perfect to Follow It

As a teenager, most of the major decisions of life were still in front on me. I would earnestly pray that God would reveal his will and guide every decision I was to make. I had been told that God had a perfect plan for my life, developed long before I was born, and it was my job to follow the clues and guideposts that came my way in order to make decisions that were in keeping with the plan. However, if I made a mistake, the perfect plan would be off the table and I would be relegated to God's second or third best plan. I prayed furiously and fearfully about each decision I made so that I would somehow maintain God's favor. It was a terrible way to live. If Jesus came that we might have life more abundantly (John 10:10b), I was certainly out of the loop.

I was talking with my advisor in college about my choice of major, fearing that I would make a mistake and forfeit God's will for my life. He asked me to look up Isaiah 30:21 and consider its meaning: Whether you turn to the right or to the left, your ears will hear a voice behind you, saying, "This is the way; walk in it." Several words literally jumped off the page: *Whether* you turn to the right or the left—this *is* the way—*walk*! It was a liberating moment for me. Whether I turned to the right or the left, I was still walking in the way. What an assuring thought!

I am well aware that this passage in Isaiah, the entire book for that matter, was not written particularly for me or to me or about me, but the words did speak to me, nonetheless. They made sense. I was to use the gifts God had given me—a keen mind, supportive parents, wise mentors, and good friends—to discern as best I could what major to pursue, but God wouldn't abandon me if I chose psychology over chemistry. Finding God's will was not some kind of spiritual scavenger hunt. On the contrary, when we think about God's will for our lives, the best place to start looking is at the intersection of our abilities and our opportunities. God does clearly guide us, and sometimes speaks directly to us, but God's leading is usually placed within the context of our lives. There is no such thing as a perfect plan that will be forfeited with our first mistake. If that were the case, we would all be lost.

* * *

I trust that you can see how the truth has flowered in my life through study, meditation, prayer, good friends, wise counsel, and experience—good, bad and ugly. If love rejoices with the truth, as Paul tells us, we should, too.

Scripture

If you have been reading through this book or even just this chapter, I trust that it is clear to you that I love Scripture. I read the Bible faithfully, prayerfully, and carefully each morning, I meditate on what I read throughout the day, and I incorporate what seems relevant in my writings. The Bible is life-giving to me, and I hope it is for you.

At the same time, over the years I have encountered some very strange, wacky, even dangerous interpretations and theologies drawn from the Bible that would make the hair on the back of my neck stand at attention, and I know that throughout history, wars, murders, bombings, torture, slavery, and a multitude of other atrocities have been carried out in the name of God and were claimed to be at the bidding of the Scriptures. It is a temptation for all of us to make the Bible tell us what we already believe or justify the condemnation of the things we hate. That's why I try to avoid proof texting, a practice of deciding what beliefs we should have about God or others, and then searching through the Bible to find a verse or two or a story that seems to justify them. Some call it mining for biblical truths, but when we ignore or haven't a clue about the context—who wrote the text, when it was written, why was it written, under what circumstances, to whom was it written, and to what end—let alone questions of history, language, translation, interpretation, and cultural settings, we tend to mine for our own planted treasures.

LOVE REJOICES WITH THE TRUTH

The Apostle John began his Gospel by referring to Jesus as the Word: "In the beginning was the Word, and the Word was with God, and the Word was God" (John 1:1), and continued, "The Word became flesh and made his dwelling among us . . . full of grace and truth" (1:14). It was the Word (Jesus) who was full of grace and truth, not the words. Now please hear me. I am not trying to diminish the power of Scripture. In fact, I am using Scripture to make my point, and my point is this: we are to worship the Word, not the words. It is the Word who is filled with grace and truth, and God knows we need both.

In the following section, Next Steps, I will offer some very practical suggestions that will help us read the Bible in context and avoid the pitfalls of picking and choosing what we want to hear and believe. It is a constant challenge for all of us, but if we walk together, there are ways to avoid at least the biggest potholes in the road.

Next Steps

When someone asks this question, "What does the Bible say about that?" they are usually making a statement in the form of a question, often presupposing the answer, regardless of what the "that" is. In truth, the Bible does not offer off-the-rack, wholesale answers for complex questions, nor should it. The Bible is the most powerful and profound collection of writings that I have ever read, and its truths continue to bl+-ossom as I read, study, discuss, and meditate on them each day. Here are a few starters for those of us who want to read with care and reverence, but also want to read with wisdom and discernment. It is a wonderful way to rejoice with the truth.

Learn About the Bible

Take some time to learn how the Bible as we know it today came to be. It is a fascinating story of inspiration, courage, and faith, and some power and politics, too. Who decided what books would be included in the Bible and what books and letters and histories would be excluded? How were these decisions made, and when? What was the social, political, and religious context of these decisions? And why are there so many different versions and translations today? Each one has its own story. Getting a sense of the history of the Bible is intriguing in and of itself, and it will aid our daily study and meditations as we faithfully seek to hear what God is saying to us today.

Select a Version to Read Daily

I think it is helpful to select a translation or version of the Bible that you like and use it regularly. It will aid in your familiarity and memorization of passages that have particular power for you, passages that speak to you and move you to faith and action. It is helpful to be mindful that the intent of some translations is to be faithful to the exact interpretation of the language of origin or a subsequent translation, while other translations and versions seek to be faithful to the intent or imagery of the text but not necessarily to be a literal word-for-word translation. This approach seeks to make the Bible accessible and understandable to the modern reader, particularly for those who are new to the faith. These differences are important to remember when we read the Bible, and both approaches have a place in our daily spiritual practices.

Read Other Versions Too

It may strike you as a contradiction to read that you should use other versions of the Bible right after I suggested that you should select one particular version or translation and read it regularly. Remember, however, that reading a version *regularly* and reading a version *exclusively* are two different things. Reading regularly from one version has many benefits, some of which were mentioned in the preceding paragraph, but reading only one version has limitations, too.

Remember the different descriptions of how we rejoice *in* the truth, or is it *with* the truth, or *in the flowering* of truth? Different translations give each of us the opportunity to consider different and expanded possibilities about what certain passages mean and have to say to us, and sometimes different translations seem to be in tension. That's okay, too. I have come to believe that learning to hold ideas, understandings, and personal beliefs in tension is a spiritual practice of great benefit. Even the Apostle Paul confessed to the church in Corinth that he didn't see and know everything. No one does. That's good to keep in mind regardless of what translation we use.

Don't Try to Read Beginning to End

I have several friends who pride themselves on telling others how many times they have read the Bible through from Genesis to Revelation, as if there was a prize for doing so. And I know of several calendar plans for reading the entire Bible through in a year. While it can be done, it seems to me that it is a bit like reading an encyclopedia through from beginning to end. The encyclopedia is astonishingly helpful, but it isn't a novel. Neither is the Bible, although there are many wonderful stories to examine, along with poems, songs, histories, prophesies, and much, much more. It's okay to be selective when you read. Choose one of the Gospels or one of the Apostle Paul's letters from the New Testament, or a group of the Psalms from the Old Testament. Another helpful practice is to follow the lectionary, a daily reading plan with a New Testament reading, an Old Testament reading, a Gospel reading, and several Psalms. If you do, you will read different portions of the Scriptures each day alone with Christians around the world, and you can find devotionals that follow the lectionary as well that provide insight and opportunities to reflect and meditate on the readings.

If you choose to read a book of the Bible, first do a little investigation about the book—who wrote it, when, to whom, and for what purpose. Did you know that Mark was the first Gospel to be written, then Matthew, Luke, and John, or that each book was written with a different audience in mind and for a different reason? And they all were preceded by the Pauline letters. So, when Paul was writing to the church in Corinth (Corinthians) or to the Christians in Rome (Romans), for example, they didn't have the Gospels to refer to for insight and instruction because they weren't written yet. And did you know that the John who wrote Revelation isn't the same person who wrote the Gospel John, or that to this day we don't know who wrote the book of Hebrews (although there are many theories)? On one level, these are interesting questions for conversations over coffee, but they are more than that. Considering such questions pushes us to think about the context of the books and passages of the Bible we read. As I firmly believe, without context we can easily get lost in the weeds and lose our way.

Don't Read Alone

Finally, many of us have the idea that reading the Bible is a solo activity, and there are certainly many benefits for getting away, being quiet, and studying the Scriptures, but if we are to rejoice in the flowering of the truth, we really do need each other. As you read and study, talk to your pastor, a good friend or two, a spiritual director, or a wise mentor about what you are reading and thinking. And there are those who have given their entire adult lives to the study of Scripture, and they write, speak, and blog on a regular basis. Seek them out. Join the conversation. As I began to write this book, I read five books on the life of Paul, and particularly as it related to his work with the Corinthian church. The five authors didn't always agree, but they were extremely helpful as I tried to understand the context of 1 Corinthians 13. As it turns out, reading the Bible is a communal act.

Conclusion

Let's be honest, when church life is messy, the truth often gets lost in the shuffle or at least tossed to the side, especially when there are controversies over theology or about church policies and practices regarding such things as the role of women in ministry, the facts of the creation, the right time or style of worship, to whom membership is extended and leadership is granted, or even if drums are permitted on the platform. Regardless of the position on these and other issues, the Bible is quoted as the authoritative source. And that's just my point. If opposing positions on almost any issue can be justified by scriptural passages, then the truth must be more than a set of stone tablets that we all read and understand the same way. Rather, the truth flowers—it is alive and growing, and we are growing into it. If we are to rejoice with it, we must offer hospitality, tolerance, grace, and space to those who read and understand Scripture differently. No one has a monopoly on the truth. No one.

And in our own embrace of Scripture, context is critical to our spiritual growth and understanding. It is good to read consistently from a particular translation, but also read and compare with other versions. Such comparisons offer great insight, as do conversations with others. While we often read the Bible alone, I have come to believe that understanding often comes through conversations with others, especially with those who read and understand things differently. As it turns out, the serious embrace of Scripture is a communal act. Love rejoices with the truth—with the flowering of the truth—and when the church is in a mess, such rejoicing is love at its best when it is needed most.

Questions for Reflection and Discussion:

1. What translation of the Bible do you read regularly? Why? Do you ever consult other versions and commentaries? Why or why not?

2. Can you think of a popular Bible verse or portion of text that is often quoted, but taken completely out of context? Why is context important?

3. What do you make of the Apostle Paul's admission in 1 Corinthians 13:12 that he sees and knows only in part (he doesn't know everything),

but someday . . . ? Does this influence how you read Paul's instructions to the ancient churches and Christians of his day?

4. Do you have someone or a small group with whom you regularly discuss your reading of Scripture? If not, how could you start such a conversation?

5. What implications does the idea that love rejoices in the flowering of the truth have for us as we strive to read Scripture faithfully, carefully, and prayerfully?

Love is patient, love is kind. It does not envy, it does not boast, it is not proud. It does not dishonor others, it is not self-seeking, it is not easily angered, it keeps no record of wrongs. Love does not delight in evil but rejoices with the truth. . . .

— 12 —

Love Always Protects

As the mountains surround Jerusalem, so the Lord
surrounds his people both now and forevermore.

—Psalm 125:2

Introduction

Love always protects. What a simple yet profound statement. I have come to believe that love is the most powerful thing in the entire world. I read in the news about a mother who jumped into the deep end of a swimming pool and pushed her young son to the side of the pool in order to save his life. Sadly, she drowned while doing so. She could not swim. Now I ask you: what in the world would motivate someone who was deathly afraid of the water and could not swim to willingly jump into the deep end of a large swimming pool? Only one thing—love. Love always protects, even at great personal cost. That's what *always* means.

This is the first of four "always" chapters. Love always protects, always trusts, always hopes, always perseveres—always. This is not the kind of love that turns tail and runs when difficulties arise or only shows itself when it is convenient to do so. No, this kind of love can be counted on to be present, to be tenacious, to be steadfast. And when church life is messy, it is one of the few things that we can count on, and it is one of the things that we are called upon to practice by showing patience, kindness, hope, and trust in our community of faith, in others, and in ourselves. My prayer is that we, all of us, will have an "always" person or two to walk with us during life's difficult times, and I pray that we will be "always" persons for others, too.

Protection

When I think about protection, being protected from something or from someone comes to mind—a heavy coat to protect from the cold, a high fence to protect from intruders, a bodyguard to keep danger away, or an insurance policy to protect if disaster comes. It is good to note, however, that insurance does not protect from disasters of one kind or another, but it can protect from financial losses when they occur. Protection sometimes prevents; at other times, it restores or makes things whole again. At the end of the day, it is unclear which kind of protection is more valuable. What is clear, however, is that both kinds of protection are needed as we journey home.

Sometimes, we need *protection from* certain toxic situations or individuals. My wife applied for a job at a local church, but the hiring process became so confusing and political that she withdrew her application. This was painful because she had high hopes that the position would be an ideal opportunity to use her gifts to minister to others. However, just a few months later, a controversy erupted and the church literally blew up and split apart. The staff left, everyone was angry, and many were deeply wounded. Some still are. As we look back at those sad events, it is clear that she was protected from an impossible situation, and for that we give thanks every day. Sometimes protection comes in the form of unanswered prayers.

Sometimes protection from danger or trouble comes to us face to face. My mother would often confront my brothers and me about the friends we kept. Of course, we were expected to be kind and friendly to everyone, but we were cautioned in no uncertain terms against "running around with those who were up to no good," as she put it. We knew what she meant, and she was right. And when church life gets messy, it is easy to get caught up in the drama. It is important to have people who look after us, watch out for us, and look us directly in the eyes and speak up when we're headed in the wrong direction with the wrong crowd. Sadly, a messy church seems to be an open invitation to those "who are up to no good." We all need protection from such situations. Sometimes the Holy Spirit speaks directly to us about these matters, but in my experience the Holy Spirit usually speaks through those who love us and care for us. Protection from difficulties is grace at work, and particularly so when it is protection from our own stubbornness and poor choices.

However, sometimes we find ourselves in the middle of a church mess. Protection *from* would have been nice, but we're already in the swamp or the swarm. We need protection *while* we navigate our way through the mess, and thankfully that's available, too. One of the most prevalent and malicious forms of misbehavior in messy situations is gossip. It seems that controversy, whether it be about theological understandings, political decisions, or personal actions, destabilizes the church. The glue that holds the community of faith together is weakened, and gossip finds its way in through the cracks and fissures. The integrity, image, and reputation of fellow believers are attacked and damaged, and sometimes ours is, too. It is in the midst of such terrible and tragic situations that we must remind ourselves that love always protects—always. We don't join in the fray, although it is tempting to do so, because that only escalates the problem. Instead, we let our response to such ugliness serve as the glue that holds the church community together. Some translations put it this way: Love bears all things (ESV). Love doesn't approve of all things or respond in kind to all things—but bears all things. We stand firm and bear them; we carry them, pray about them, refuse to join in, and go on loving in the middle of the mess. And where is God when all this is going on? Right there in the mess with us, working to bring healing, hope, and wholeness.

So, since love always protects (bears all things), so do we. It isn't an easy road to walk but it is the right one. Sometimes in God's great love and mercy, we are *protected from* a church in a mess, and sometimes in God's great love and mercy, we are *protected while* in the church mess. It isn't a role that any of us would choose or cherish, but when we are called to be the glue that holds things together, we step up and lean in, knowing that we never serve or suffer alone. God's providence and protection are with us, now and always.

Scripture

When I think about accounts from the Bible, it is tempting to start with the stories about Daniel and his face-off in the lion's den, and the three young men in the fiery furnace, both found in the Old Testament book of Daniel. I can't remember a year in Sunday school or a Summer Bible School that Daniel and his three friends didn't make an appearance. They are evergreen stories about their faith in God and how God protected them. As a child, I often imagined what I would do if I suddenly found myself in a lion's den because of my faith. I prayed that I would have the courage of Daniel. As it turns out, I have found myself in a lion's den a time to two, and I can attest that God was faithful, even when the trouble was of my own making. I must also attest, however, that unlike Daniel, I didn't come through those situations totally unscathed. I've come to believe that the point of the stories in Daniel isn't that God will always jump in and miraculously save us from all suffering because of our faith, but rather that God is in the mess with us, whether we suffer or are delivered from harm in unimagined ways.

The other reason that I am hesitant to use the story of Daniel and his friends is that modern scholars are inclined to see Daniel as more of a legendary figure whose prowess gained scope and power over the years. Honestly, we don't know if all the events reported in Daniel actually happened. Maybe they did; maybe they didn't. I'll leave that up to you to decide. However, given my comments about rejoicing *with the flowering* of truth in the last chapter, I must say here that some of the Bible stories we have heard since childhood may need to be revisited. I heard a Native American wisdom keeper once say as a way of introducing his speech: "I am going to tell you a story. Now, it didn't all happen, but it is a true story." I would say the same thing about the story of Daniel and the lion's den. I don't know how it went down or even if it went down, but it is a true story, nonetheless. That is to say, Daniel has much to teach us about faith, courage, and devotion in the midst of difficulties.

Let's look instead at two other stories. What follows are two examples of divine protection found in the New Testament, one about Mary and Joseph and the other about the Apostle Paul. As you will see, one is a case of *protection while;* the other is a case when *protection from* might have been ignored. We will start with the events surrounding the birth of Jesus.

Mary and Joseph: Matthew 1:18–24

The story of Mary and Joseph is familiar to most of us. Matthew 1 tells us that Mary and Joseph were pledged to be married, but "Mary was found to be pregnant" (18). Imagine Joseph's shock and anger, and in that time and culture he had every right to wash his hands of the relationship, walk away, and leave Mary to deal on her own with the public shame and embarrassment (19). But an angel appeared to Joseph in a dream and told him that he shouldn't be afraid to take Mary as his wife. There were big plans in the works for the child (20–22). When Joseph awoke from the dream, he did exactly what he was told to do, even though the law and righteous indignation were on his side (24), and in doing so, he protected Mary from the public shame of an apparent moral failure.

Nine months later when Jesus was born in Bethlehem, Joseph had a second visit from an angel. This time he was instructed to take the baby and mother to Egypt. It wasn't safe to stay (13). After the long trip from Nazareth to Bethlehem and the labor and birth in a stable, it was probably the last thing he wanted to hear. They must have been exhausted, and the baby was so young and fragile. Still, Joseph got up and they left that night, and none too soon. When the Roman troops arrived, they were already gone (14).

When word came to Joseph in a dream, he obeyed, even if it didn't make sense at the time. He took steps of faith in the dark, and he gave and received protection in the middle of a mess. I know we all want to hear God's voice and receive protection from and while we navigate the messes we face. Such guidance is truly a gift, but sometimes it is difficult to identify God's voice in the cacophony of voices that cry out to be heard: "Do you know what you should do? You should . . ." And sometimes it is our own stubbornness that gets in the way, as in the case of the Apostle Paul and his desire to return to Jerusalem.

Paul's Trip to Jerusalem and Rome: Acts 19–21

While in Ephesus, Paul announced that "in the Spirit" he made a decision to go first to Jerusalem, then on to Rome (Acts 19:21). This was late in his ministry, and he had preached a lot, seen a lot, and experienced a lot, including great highs like the conversion of new believers and the start of new churches along with the lows of rejection, treachery, arrest, mockery, and beatings, to name just a few. He knew that Jerusalem was not a safe place, but he was adamant that this was the right time to go and the right place to be, so go he did. Along the way, his friends, fellow workers, and faithful disciples wept and begged him not to go (20:37; 21:4). It was simply too dangerous, but Paul dismissed their concerns and made his way to Jerusalem where he was promptly and predictably arrested. From there, he did make his way to Rome, but as a prisoner awaiting trial. There, most likely, he was killed during one of the purges of Christians by the Romans. No one knows for sure.

Clearly, Paul's trip to Rome was full of opportunities to witness to officials along the way, and I am sure that God was honored by Paul's ministry, but I can't help wondering if Paul's stubborn insistence to go to Jerusalem over the caution of those who loved him and ministered with him might have prematurely ended Paul's work. I know that he wanted to go to Spain. He wrote to the Christians in Rome that he had exhausted his opportunities for ministry where he was at and would visit them on the way to Spain (Rom 15:23–24). There is no biblical evidence that he ever made it.

What would have happened if Paul had listened to the counsel of those who loved him and ministered with him, pleading with him not to go? The disciples in Tyre urged him "through the Spirit" to change plans, but he pressed on (Acts 21:4), and Luke records that "we" and the people in Caesarea pleaded with him to change his mind (21:10–12). Now please hear me. I am not questioning Paul's ministry or his passion or his desire to be faithful to God's call and direction, but I do wonder if given his desire to go to Spain, he might have traveled to Rome by another way. I know there have been times when I ignored the concerns shared by close friends, and as I look back, I see that they were right. I ignored their wise counsel because I thought I knew better, but I didn't. Surely, God did not leave or forsake me, but I unnecessarily walked down some lonely, bumpy roads because I ignored the danger signs sent my way. I ignored those who were trying to protect me, mostly from myself. I wonder if Paul did the same. I'll let you decide.

Next Steps

Before we close this chapter, I want to offer three simple steps that you can take to sidestep some of the emotional toll that comes when your church is in a mess. Such situations will drain your spirit, and they can be hurtful, too. So, how do we abide in a love that always protects? The first step is to take some time to reflect, to *look back* at how God and others have offered protection from and protection while you were in a mess, when your life was in the ditch. It is easy to forget love's track record. Looking back and remembering the faithfulness of God's love and the care of others fosters a deep sense of gratitude and a humble confidence that things will work out. You are not alone, and what you are navigating is not life threatening. Love will see you through and bid you home.

As you take time to reflect back and express gratitude for and gain confidence from the protection that has been extended to you in your own messy times, a second step is to *look around* for those who need protection now. It may be that you can offer "protection from" by expressing a word of concern or caution, or it may be that you can offer "protection while" by walking with someone who is in a mess, even if it is of their own making. Pray for eyes to see and ears to hear others who need to hear from you. Be the love that always protects.

And finally, *look forward* with confidence that: "As the mountains surround Jerusalem, so the LORD surrounds his people both now and forevermore" (Ps 125:2). When Paul wrote to the Christians in Corinth that love always protects, I think he was saying much the same thing. This love does not guarantee that all will be rosy in life; that wouldn't be life. But it does promise that whatever we face, wherever we go, we are surrounded by God's love. We never journey alone.

Conclusion

This is the first of four "always" chapters: Love always protects, always trusts, always hopes, always perseveres. What a wonderful promise, and what an enormous challenge for all of us who want to be agents of love in a church mess of one kind or another. Sometimes we are protected *from* hurtful situations, and sometimes we are protected *while* in the mess. The promise isn't that we will never suffer or be hurt, but that God will be with us in the midst of the mess, working for good. We are never alone. And we know that suffering will change us, and it can change us for the better. We, all of us, pray that we will be faithful to the challenge of protecting others who are in the mess, even as we pray to be protected by God's love—the most powerful thing in the world.

Questions for Reflection and Discussion:

1. As you look back on your spiritual journey, can you think of the time when you were *protected from* a toxic or dangerous situation, perhaps by a nudge from the Holy Spirit or by a word of caution from a loved one, mentor, pastor, or good friend? What was the result?

2. As you look back on your spiritual journey, can you think of the time when you were *protected while* in a mess, perhaps of your own making? How were you protected and what did you learn from that experience about God and about your own spiritual journey?

3. Can you think of a time when protection was offered to you in the form of a caution from someone, but you ignored the warning? What was the result?

4. Do you know of someone who is in a mess right now? If so, how might you walk with them through this difficult time in their journey?

5. How did you respond to the author's suggestion that the Apostle Paul might have ignored the pleas and warnings of those who walked with him and loved him very much? Could the end of Paul's life have been different?

*Love is patient, love is kind. It does not envy, it does not boast,
it is not proud. It does not dishonor others, it is not self-seeking,
it is not easily angered, it keeps no record of wrongs.
Love does not delight in evil but rejoices with the truth.
It always protects, . . .*

— 13 —

Love Always Trusts

Those who know your name will trust in you, for you, Lord,
have never forsaken those who seek you.

—Ps 9:10

Introduction

Love always trusts, Paul writes. That sounds like a tall order. Always? Does that mean that we are to trust everyone, regardless of how we have been treated by someone in the past? That is more than just a tall order—that's silly. Most of us have lived long enough to know that we can't take everyone at their word. We've lived long enough to know that many people, some very close to us, are not reliable or truthful. They don't always do what they say they will do, and they don't always say what they know to be true. And others make promises that they simply can't keep, and sadly, deep inside they knew it when the promises were made. Simply put, we can't trust everyone.

So, one question that comes to mind is: who can we trust? This is an important question, an existential question, and we'll get to it a bit later in this meditation, but it is not the first question that begs to be answered. Rather than starting by making a list of those we think we can trust, let's start by asking a more personal question: can we be trusted? Are we trustworthy? That comes a lot closer to home, doesn't it? Home is always a good place to start.

To be trustworthy is to be reliable, truthful, willing, and able to do what we say and say what we will do—and then do it! And when a church is in a mess, trust is one of the first casualties. We look around and lament that we don't know who to trust. While this may be true, sadly so, I believe the challenge of Paul's words—love always trusts, or to put it another way, love is always trustworthy—is to ask ourselves if we can be trusted. Are we trustworthy? Are we reliable? Do we show up when we say we will, or do we text an excuse at the last minute? While I was growing up in a small farming community, my parents were insistent that our family always did what we said we would do, show up where expected, tell the truth, bring the cookies as promised, and return any borrowed tools on time. We didn't have much, but we had our word, our reputation, we were told, and if we lost that, we would really be poor. One of the beauties of a small community is that everyone knows you and what you do. There's a built-in accountability in that arrangement. Honestly, it made me a better person.

We were taught that it was important to keep our promises, and not make promises we couldn't keep, no matter how noble or important it made us feel at the time. "Let your word be your bond," we were told, and even though my brothers and I didn't really know what a bond was, we understood enough to know that to be trustworthy was a good way to live and the best way to love both God and neighbor.

Okay, so who can we trust, even as we do our best to be trustworthy? The psalmist had it right: "Those who know your name will trust in you, for you, Lord, have never forsaken those who seek you" (Ps 9:10). God is trustworthy—reliable, truthful, willing, and able to keep generous promises, to show up in the middle of our darkest nights, to journey with us in our deepest valleys, and to be truthful with us. When Paul wrote to the messy church in Corinth so many years ago that love was trustworthy, I believe that he was referring to the character of God. At the end of the day, every day, we can count on God, who promises much and delivers more.

And as we place our trust in God, we work diligently to be trustworthy, too. That's a real challenge, a spiritual practice, and a priceless gift we can offer to our own messy congregation. We can't always trust everyone we meet, but everyone we meet can trust us. That's up to each of us. We'll address some ways to practice being trustworthy in the Next Steps section, but first let's look at how trust played out in the life of King David, even as he faced death and his kingdom was a mess. At such a juncture, who could he trust?

Scripture

The kingdom was a mess. King David was very old, literally on his death bed. He was in his royal bed, but the covers couldn't keep him warm. He and everyone else knew that the end was near. Surely, Adonijah, one of David's sons, knew, and set about to name himself as David's successor. When word got back to David, he knew he needed to act fast to counter this grab for power, and in order to keep his promise to Bathsheba to make their son, Solomon, king, he summoned Zadok the priest, Nathan the prophet, and Benaiah son of Jehoiada to his bedside. They were to take Solomon to Gihon, and there anoint him as David's successor. The coup was eventually quelled, and Solomon consolidated his power and his kingdom (1 Kgs 1–2). The rest, as they say, is history.

When David decided it was time to send Solomon to Gihon to be anointed king, he obviously needed to surround Solomon with people who could be trusted. So, why Zadok, Benaiah, and Nathan? The short answer is that they had proven to be trustworthy. The long answer will take a bit of unpacking. First, let's take Zadok, the high priest. He was high priest at the time of the rebellion of David's son, Absalom. He offered to take the ark of the covenant and follow David into the hills as he fled from the revolt, but David asked him to stay in Jerusalem instead. Hopefully, he would return someday. He stayed, and David did return. During the revolt, Zadok proved that he was loyal, even as he himself faced death (2 Sam 15:24–29). He was trustworthy.

The story of Nathan the prophet is a bit more familiar to most of us. David had a fling with Bathsheba, even though she was a married woman, and when she found out that she was pregnant, David tried first to trick her husband, Uriah, a soldier, into thinking that it was his baby, and having failed at that, he had Uriah moved to the fiercest point of the fighting where he was killed in battle. This didn't sit well with Nathan, so he came to confront King David, which in and of itself was risky business—still is. Power rarely enjoys being confronted. David could have simply ignored Nathan, sent him off in exile, or had him executed, but instead was humbled by the confrontation and ashamed and repentant about his sin (2 Sam 12:1–15). If David knew anything about Nathan, he knew that he was a person who told the truth, all the time—to anyone, even the king. He was trustworthy.

But what about Benaiah? Why did David trust him? I think there's a clue in one of my favorite verses in the Bible: "Benaiah son of Jehoiada, a valiant fighter from Kabzeel, performed great exploits. He struck down Moab's two mightiest warriors. He also went down into a pit on a snowy day and killed a lion" (2 Sam 23:20). Obviously, Benaiah was a real fighter, having struck down not one but Moab's two mightiest warriors. Two against one are not good odds in any fight, but Benaiah carried the day. He knew how to fight and could hold his own, but there's more. He went down into a pit on a snowy day and killed a lion. Wow! First of all, I wouldn't fight a lion anywhere if I had a chance to pass. Second, if I had to face a lion with a spear, it wouldn't be in a pit with limited escape routes available. And finally, if I had to face a lion in a pit, I would wait until my footing was more secure. Surely it wouldn't be on a snowy day. But that's exactly what Benaiah did. He went down into a pit on a snowy day and killed a lion. Why? No one knows for sure, but I think that Benaiah went into the pit to fight the lion because that's where the lion was—and that's what he was trained to do. That was his job, and he was willing and able to do his duty when called upon. He was trustworthy, too.

Thus, Zadok, the reliable one, Nathan, the truthful one, and Benaiah, the willing and able one, were summoned to the palace and appointed to escort Solomon to the place where he would be anointed king. They were entrusted with the young king's life because they had earned David's trust. So, how do we earn and display trust in the middle of a messy church situation where there is little reason to trust anyone? In what follows, several small steps for building trust will be discussed. As with most spiritual practices, small steps are necessary to make big strides.

Next Steps

Trust is so fleeting, so delicate. So is trusting someone. We all want to be able to trust our friends, our families, and those with whom we worship each week, and we want to be trusted, too. We want to be trustworthy. Here are four rather simple-sounding steps that will send us on a spiritual journey—a journey to be real, to be more authentic, to be holy. It is a long journey, but a good one.

Show Up

Take a moment and do some honest evaluation and introspection. Do you show up when you say you will? Do you follow through on your commitments? Can others count on you, even when you are tired, over-extended, lose interest, or receive a better offer? It is so easy to rationalize that we won't be missed, we're not really needed, or other things have come up that are more important. I know, I've done it myself. But at the end of the day, if we want to be trusted, our word has to mean something more than just showing up when it is convenient. I'll bet that we can all think of someone who, when they tell you that they will be there, wherever there is, you don't count on it because they simply don't always show up—and their excuses are miserable. You don't trust them because they are not reliable. At the end of the day, we have to look in the mirror and ask: Am I reliable? Do I show up no matter what? The first small step in earning trust is to be there—every single time. An excuse, no matter how creative, is really no substitute.

Tell the Truth

I want to be cautious here. We don't have to say everything we think or tell everything we know, and when church life is in a mess, there is certainly much that can and should go unsaid. However, there are times when we are asked a direct question or invited to speak into a discussion about an impending decision that impacts the entire congregation. In those instances, the truth as you see it is invited and often required. Sharing can be difficult, and it should always be done with humility, but sometimes someone has to say what everyone else is thinking. Have you ever spoke up at a meeting, and afterward been thanked (usually in private) for speaking up, sharing what was on everyone's mind? Sometimes you have to give the community voice. So, swallow hard and speak the truth. This is particularly important when, like the prophet Nathan, the truth is corrective, and a price may be paid for speaking out or into someone's life. Beware of anyone who loves to be the prophet. It's not a comfortable or enjoyable role, but think of those times when someone spoke into your life and challenged your behavior or attitudes. Be trustworthy and speak the truth—kindly, carefully, and humbly.

Keep Your Promises, and Don't Make Promises You Can't or Won't Keep

If we want to be trustworthy, we need to show up, tell the truth, and keep our promises. Since our word is our bond, if we say we'll do something, we just do it. It's that simple, or is it? Sometimes our problem is follow-through, and sadly at other times, we make promises we never intended to keep in the first place. Just ask anyone who raises funds for churches or other not-for-profit organizations about those who promise big gifts, receive some attention for doing so, and then walk away and never give a dime past the first installment. It was all for show—big hat, no cattle, as my father was fond of saying. If we want to be counted as trustworthy, we must be careful about what we promise to do, and then be sure to follow through on our promises. Intentions are nice, but without execution, intention is just an ugly form of procrastination.

Stop, Look, and Listen

Finally, if we desire to be counted as trustworthy, think about persons who have shown themselves to be trustworthy with you, and intentionally spend time with them. Talk to them and walk with them. Watch them. Listen to them. Learn from them. I truly believe that we are shaped by the people we spend time with, so if we want to be trustworthy, identify those who you see as trustworthy and let them speak into your life by word and example. Share your own challenges with them. Rather than running away, they are more likely to say, "Me too." No one gets it all right the first time.

* * *

These next steps may seem to be simple and self-evident, and on one level they are. Spiritual formation is not rocket science. On another level, however, it is the constant practice of daily mini steps that take us on a long spiritual journey. If we start each day with serious intent to be trustworthy—consistently showing up, telling the truth, even when it is painful to do so, and keeping our promises—we are on the way to spiritual growth and renewal, even in the midst of a mess at church. As we place our trust in God, we offer ourselves to be shaped and formed in holy ways, in the very image of God, who has never forsaken us. If we know anything, we know this: God is love, and love is trustworthy—always.

Conclusion

Love always trusts, Paul tells us, and when we encounter a messy church situation, the first question we think about is this: Who can I trust? Of course, that's an important question, but a better place to start is with these questions: Can I be trusted? Am I trustworthy? In the midst of the mess, we can't control all that is going on, but we do have agency over what we say and do. We can choose to be trustworthy and demonstrate it by our own actions.

Love always trusts seems like an impossible standard since we all know that not everyone can be trusted and it is not wise to act as if everyone can be trusted, even in church. Perhaps a better way to understand Paul's description of trust is this: love is always trustworthy. We can take that to the bank. We know that to be trustworthy is to be dependable, truthful, and willing and able to keep our promises. We saw these attributes in the lives of Zadok, the dependable high priest; Nathan, the truthful prophet; and Benaiah, the courageous soldier. The aging king, David, under siege and at the end of his days, knew that they could be trusted.

May we take stock of our own lives. Do we do what we say we will do? Do we speak the truth, even when it is not popular or comfortable? And do we keep the promises and not make promises that we can't or won't keep? In other words, do we live lives of integrity? At the end of the day, if love is always trustworthy, then we are challenged to live that way, too. It is through a series of small steps that the journey to wholeness and holiness makes its way.

Questions for Reflection and Discussion:

1. Can you think of someone who is simply unreliable? You can't trust them to show up and bring the dessert as promised? What does this say about that person, and how do you deal with this behavior?

2. Have you ever shared at a meeting, and then had others come to you after the meeting and thank you for expressing what they were all thinking or feeling? Why do you think they didn't speak up, and what does it say about the atmosphere that others wouldn't?

3. Can you think of someone who broke a promise to you? How did you respond, and what if you found out that the promise maker had no intention to fulfill the promise in the first place? What would that do to your relationship?

4. If you were honest, what is most challenging for you: showing up, speaking the truth, or keeping your promises? What first steps could you take to address this challenge, understanding that these are spiritual practices?

5. Love always trusts. That seems difficult to imagine since we know that we can't trust everyone, and if we are honest, we're not always trustworthy either. Is it helpful to think about Paul's words this way: Love is always trustworthy, and to understand that it refers to the character of God, not our friends or ourselves?

Love is patient, love is kind. It does not envy, it does not boast,
it is not proud. It does not dishonor others, it is not self-seeking,
it is not easily angered, it keeps no record of wrongs.
Love does not delight in evil but rejoices with the truth.
It always protects, always trusts, . . .

— 14 —

Love Always Hopes

Yes, my soul, find rest in God; my hope comes from him.

—Ps 62:5

Introduction

I₉ faith sends us on a spiritual journey, it is hope that keeps us going until we find home. In this chapter, we'll look a bit closer at the spiritual power of hope and try to understand why the Apostle Paul declared that love always hopes, particularly when church is a mess. Honestly, there isn't much else to hold the congregation together during tough and especially terrible times. Hope, as it turns out, is both the fuel that keeps us on the journey and the glue that holds us together as we go. Before we look a bit closer at hope and hoping, I want to share a story of Christmas hope.

Hoping for Snow

When I was twelve, I received a weather station from my parents as a Christmas present, capable of measuring temperature, wind speed, barometric pressure, and humidity (well, sort of). I had hopes of becoming a weatherman, working for a local TV station in Saginaw, that is until my least favorite uncle came for Christmas dinner. He took joy in unkindly teasing and embarrassing his nephews, and this occasion was no exception. In a loud voice in front of the entire crew (about twenty-five family members) he asked me for a prediction: "Since you are so smart now with your new weather station, when will it snow? We want a prediction." All eyes were on me, and I felt my face getting red and the back of neck getting hot. I didn't know what to do, but from somewhere deep inside these words spilled out,

"It will snow before three o'clock today!" "Really," my uncle retorted, "we'll see how good of a weatherman you are."

That last statement ruined my entire day. From eleven o'clock on, my uncle asked each half hour, "Is it snowing yet?" with a not-so-nice grin. "Not yet," I would say, and kept looking to the west, hoping for any sign of snow. There was none—mostly clear skies. The waiting was terribly painful, and the closer it got to three o'clock, the worse I felt. This was certainly not the Christmas I had anticipated.

Honestly, I nearly lost all hope. Then a miracle happened. Just a few minutes before three, some tiny snowflakes came drifting down, looking more like ashes from a campfire than a snowstorm. It wasn't much, and it didn't last very long, but I confidently declared it to be a snowfall. The family didn't protest, and we all sat down for Christmas dinner. Somehow my spirit was renewed, and Christmas had been saved.

I learned a few lessons that day. To begin with, hoping and waiting are really hard. They test your spirit, especially so when the stakes are high—like hoping the latest lab test results bring back good news, or waiting the phone to ring after a job interview, or praying for someone to make it home in the midst of a bad storm, and for a fragile young boy, for it to start snowing before three o'clock in the afternoon on Christmas day. Hoping isn't always easy, but I have come to believe that it is an honest act of faith, a prayer for what we do not yet see. And it can be a spiritual practice, too, shaping us in ways known and unknown.

And I learned to believe in miracles. Now I realize that predicting snow in Michigan in late December is not going out too much of a limb, but the skies were mostly clear that day. Of course, it could have been just a lucky coincidence. I grant you that. But then again, could it be that the God of the universe saw a little boy hoping and waiting and praying for snow in the face of ridicule, embarrassment, and shame, and decided to send just a few tiny snowflakes his way? I honestly believe that's what happened. Albert Einstein is quoted as saying that you either have to believe that nothing is a miracle or that everything is. I tend to go with the latter.

To this very day, I smile every time I see falling snow, acknowledging all the snowflakes in my life—the remembered and forgotten signs of hope, the manifestations of God's love and grace.

Hoping

Hope can be a verb (we are hoping for something) or a noun (we place our hope in something). Hoping, something we do, can be akin to wishing, as when I hoped for snow fall by three on Christmas day. Honestly, I didn't have much faith that it would snow, but I wished as hard as I could; I wanted it to happen, and I almost lost all hope. When we find ourselves in a mess at church, and that is most of us at one time or another, what is it that we are hoping for? Let me suggest just three, and as you will see, they take us in different directions.

When church life is messy, some of us are hoping for restoration, for things to be as they once were, for the good old days we remember to return. I am thinking of a small church on the edge of a modest town. The young pastor is working very hard to bring life and renewal to a community of faith after the ugly departure of the lead pastor. It hasn't been easy. He has his hands full dealing with mistrust, gossip, fear, anger, and disillusionment. Even though it is a small congregation, he faces deep organizational and relational challenges. However, his biggest problem in the congregation is a retired minister who is his constant critic of little things—the order of service, the lighting of candles, the placement of the pastoral prayer, the songs that are sung, when people arrive, and how the greeters are dressed, to name just a few—and the solution to all his concerns is for that little church to do things the way it was done in his own ministerial heyday, even though it was in another part of the country, in a large city, in a different social context, and more than forty years ago! He hopes for restoration, a return to the way church used to be—or so as he remembers it to be, and rather than being the young pastor's biggest encourager, he is his biggest critic and a constant demotivator. This is not love at its best.

Some of us are hoping for renewal, to make everything new, to change everything—particularly as we want church to be. Rather than a return to the glory days, this is a hope that the church can be remade anew in our own idea of what church should be, particularly the music, the preaching style, and the guiding theology. Last year, I welcomed a new couple at the church where I attended and volunteered. After the first week, they volunteered to lead the prayer team, sing on the worship team, sit on the board, and fill in for the pastor if needed. And after a month or so, they shared with me that the church was not biblical enough, meaning that the pastor did not stand in front of the congregation with a big black Bible in one hand while gesturing and pointing at the congregation with the other. And although they granted that the Bible was read carefully, thoughtfully, and prayerfully, it was not read literally—word by word. All this had to change. They were also concerned that women were allowed to serve on the pastoral team, preach, and even be ordained. That had to change. And they were adamant that an altar call needed to be extended each Sunday and a much greater emphasis given to evangelism each week, because the role of the church was to save souls, period, not to assist those in financial or physical need. That had to change, too.

As kindly as I could, I told the couple that while they had joined our faith community, they were insisting that the church become something altogether different from what it was and intended to be. There might be congregations around that would fit their idea of a faithful church, but it wasn't us, nor would it be. If these were their non-negotiables, they needed to attend elsewhere. If they stayed, they would only add to the mess. They hoped for renewal, but only on their own terms. Love at its best does not behave that way.

A third hope is for reconciliation. In the middle of the mess, we hope and pray that frayed relationships will be strengthened and friendships can be saved. We hope to join the work of the Holy Spirit in the healing in each of us, and among us, too. We want our fellowship to be kind and life-giving, and our spirits to be renewed, not the style of worship or preaching. This is love at its best.

So, what are we hoping for—restoration, renewal, or reconciliation? Do we want to go back to the way we remember it used to be, to remake the church to serve our own set of beliefs and attitudes, or to find health and healing through reconciliation? Truly, love always hopes, but what we are hoping for makes a huge difference in the life of a messy church, and in our own lives, too.

Hope

Hope is also a noun, the glue that holds a community together and the energy that keeps us on the spiritual road as we journey toward home. It can be enormously powerful, propelling an entire congregation forward during uncertain times, but it can be fragile, too. Hope can dissipate and almost disappear when meanness and selfishness rear their ugly heads.

I believe that we all have hope for church when it is in a mess, some more than others and some more clearly than others, but all of us have some. So, the question is: where are we placing our hope? This is a question rarely expressed but terribly important if we are to find our way when church is a mess. Some of us place our hope in popularity. It isn't often admitted, especially to ourselves, but what is at work if we are honest is this: if we can be liked by everyone in the congregation, be the life of the party as it were, then we will be okay, whether or not the community is healthy. And some of us place our hope in being prominent and influential, although we couch this hope as a way for us to use our gifts. Honestly, we want to be seen on the platform and in front of the congregation. It is position and influence that we pursue, and it is rarely for the benefit of the community of faith. Placing our hope in popularity and prominence turns out to be a self-seeking, self-promoting approach when church is a mess. At the end of the day, we are called to be faithful, not to save the circus, no matter how heroic it may seem at the time.

If we place our hope in popularity and prominence, the glue does not stick. It does not hold a messy situation together, and it does little to edify ourselves. Rather, we are consumed by hopes that will not see the light of day. Particularly when church is messy, there is only one place for our hope to dwell—in the promises of God, which we carry with the confident expectation that God has always been faithful, and always will be. We place our hope in the very character of God. Love always hopes. Honestly, it is that simple, but in the middle of a mess, so hard to do.

Before we look at several Next Steps as we work faithfully to place our hope in the promises of God, let's visit two passages from Scripture that offer some insights regarding the power and the fragility of hope.

Scripture

The Apostle Paul writes to the Christians in Rome, "we know that suffering produces perseverance; perseverance, character; and character, hope" (Rom 5:3–4). Honestly, I am not fond of his message. Of course, I do want to be able to persevere, to have grit, to hold on and show up, and to develop character and hope, but I'm not crazy about the suffering part. I wish there was an easier path to hope, but if there is, I haven't found it. My father was fond of telling me when I faced difficult times, "It builds character." I suppose he was right, but I wondered just how much character I needed to develop. As it turns out, over the years I've needed all the character I could muster, and hope, too.

And Paul was not just offering a lofty theory; he knew what he was taking about. As he wrote to the church in Corinth:

> Five times I received from the Jews the forty lashes minus one. Three times I was beaten with rods, once I was pelted with stones, three times I was shipwrecked, I spent a night and a day in the open sea, I have been constantly on the move. I have been in danger from rivers, in danger from bandits, in danger from my fellow Jews, in danger from Gentiles; in danger in the city, in danger in the country, in danger at sea; and in danger from false believers. I have labored and toiled and have often gone without

sleep; I have known hunger and thirst and have often gone without food; I have been cold and naked. Besides everything else, I face daily the pressure of my concern for all the churches (2 Cor 11:24–28).

Clearly, when Paul wrote about suffering, perseverance, character, and hope, he knew what he was talking about. According to Paul, hope is not some type of fuzzy, warm, religious feeling that is passed around on Sunday morning with a smile and a hug, but rather the certainty that regardless of the trials we face, God is with us, in the mess, bringing healing and wholeness even as we suffer and hold on as best we can—even when the best we can is not very good at all. Love always hopes because we place our hope in God. That builds character, too.

And when we speak of perseverance and hope, I can't help thinking of Job, a good and faithful man who dealt with more sorrow and loss than anyone should have to experience in a lifetime, but experience it he did. He aptly summed up his situation: "For sighing has become my daily food; my groans pour out like water. What I feared has come upon me; what I dreaded has happened to me. I have no peace, no quietness; I have no rest, but only turmoil" (Job 3:24–26).

No peace, no quietness, no rest. Not a pretty picture, but rather a tragic scene from a life that has been turned on its head. He is suffering, and he's lost everything—except hope. Somehow from somewhere he has grit, if nothing else. He's a grinder. He keeps talking, keeps showing up, keeps trying to understand that which cannot be understood. He is devastated, angry, mystified, but he keeps leaning in, expressing hope beyond all hope. Sometimes that's all we can do.

So, what can we take from the experiences of Paul and Job when we find ourselves in a mess at church? Certainly, we can see that following and trusting God is no guarantee of a life of luxury. Not by any standard. We may be wounded and suffer more that we even think we can, but through the mess, we show up and lean in, we grind, becoming a living expression of the hope the keeps us together and keeps us going. It is a living expression of the belief that love always hopes.

Next Steps

So, how do we face the mess and grind on, expressing a love that always hopes? As we see from Paul and Job, we can't anticipate that each day will be a cakewalk, but we can learn to lean in and keep going. How? Let me name four small steps that will take us in the right direction.

Revisit God's Promises

When hope begins to wane in the middle of the grind and in the middle of the mess, start by revisiting God's promises in Scripture. God is a lavish promise maker, and we can count on his promises. However, as I have mentioned elsewhere in this book, it is important to distinguish between passages and promises there were made to a certain people at a certain time for a specific purpose, such as Jeremiah 29:11, a promise to bring the exiles in Babylon back to Jerusalem after seventy years (see Jer 20:10), and other promises and passages that are more inclusive in scope. For instance, Micah 6:8 was also written in a specific time and place, but I believe the call for *all mortals* to act justly, love mercy, and walk humbly with God includes us. In either case, however, we can be moved by the promises made and kept by God (even if not specifically to us) and find hope in the reality that we serve the same faithful God who makes and keeps promises to us.

And we have much to take from the stories of Abraham, Jacob, Jonah, Rahab, Mary Magdalene, and Peter, all far from perfect, about the faithfulness of God. Stories have a way of conveying meaning to each of us as we identify with them and find ourselves in them. When we fall short, perhaps especially when we fall short, we have a sustaining and empowering hope, certainly not because we are perfect, but because God is faithful. Our hope comes from God (Rom 15:13a).

Think about God's Track Record in Your Own Life

Take some time for introspection. Schedule an appointment with yourself and think back about God's faithfulness in your life. Think of times when you came up short, didn't keep your promises or tell the truth, failed to step up and lean into the mess when needed, or simply gave up and quit, yet God was there and at work in the mess and in the mess of your own life. And remarkably and unexpectedly, good came from these tough and terrible times. As a result, we see that our hope comes from God, the maker and keeper of extravagant promises. Make your own personal list of *Promises Made—Promises Kept* and put it in a place where you can see it and update it regularly. It will serve as a hopeful reminder that God has been faithful, and is at work, now and always.

Walk with Those Who Hope

Throughout this book, I have made reference to the need for each of us to have mentors, role models, spiritual directors, and a few good and faithful friends. I do so again. I have come to believe that relationships are the most formative aspect of the spiritual journey—particularly our relationship with God and with a few trusted souls whom we invite to walk with us and speak into our lives. We are influenced by and become like those we spend time with, particularly honest time, real time, hard times, sharing life together. And as we do, we gather hope, a stubborn hope that we are not alone in the dark of the night and that morning will come. Find hopeful friends and walk with them. As we do, we are shaped and formed in good and hopeful ways. Simply put, relationships matter because spiritual formation is a relational process.

Show Up and Grind

The most powerful expression of hope I know is simply to show up, to lean in and do what you can, even if you can't do much at all or there isn't much at all to do. Presence speaks volumes. It may sound simple, but it isn't. It's hard! We take our cue from Job. He was devastated, disillusioned, and downright angry with God, but he was a grinder, too. He showed up, kept engaged, and did what he could, which wasn't much at all. In the mess, the temptation is to run and hide, to close shop and go home. I've done it myself a time or two, but hope is expressed and embodied by those who set their faces like flint (Isa 50:7) and do what they can. And as it turns out, it is contagious. Others draw hope when our hope is expressed by our actions. We have all heard that actions speak louder than words. In this case, it's true.

And when we show up, we lean in and grind. We do so not with the certainty that everything will turn out like Facebook or the ending of a Disney movie. We know that real life doesn't always work that way. Rather, we come knowing that God is faithfully present, working to bring hope and healing in the mess and through the mess. We show up expressing the hope that morning will come.

Conclusion

If faith sends us on a spiritual journey, it is hope that keeps us going until we find home. Hope, as it turns out, is both the fuel that keeps us on the journey and the glue to holds us together as we go. I started this chapter with these two thoughts, and I trust that it is fitting to conclude in the same way. At the end of the day and in the middle of a dark night, hope may be the only thing that we have to hold on to, even as hope holds on to us.

When church is a mess, Paul tells us, love always hopes, and it is best expressed by just showing up, leaning in and grinding on, a tangible expression of our confidence in a God who makes extravagant promises to each of us, and keeps those promises come hell or high water. It is in this sense that hope gives rest. We dine at a table set before us in the presence of our enemies (Ps 23:5), even if the most formidable enemy we face is us. Love always hopes.

Questions for Reflection and Discussion:

1. Hope, we have read, is both the fuel for our personal journey and the glue that holds us together. Fuel and glue, personal and communal—have you experienced hope working in these two very different ways? How so?

2. When you think about church, what you are hoping for? What might happen if we focused on reconciliation rather than trying to make or remake church according to our own desires and experiences?

3. Why do we place our hope in popularity or prominence rather than in God's promises? What is at work when we do?

4. If you were to make a *God's Promises Made—Promises Kept* list, what would be the top one or two? How have these promises shaped your spiritual journey?

5. What passage or story from Scripture gives you the most hope? Explain.

Love is patient, love is kind. It does not envy, it does not boast,
it is not proud. It does not dishonor others, it is not self-seeking,
it is not easily angered, it keeps no record of wrongs.
Love does not delight in evil but rejoices with the truth.
It always protects, always trusts, always hopes, . . .

— 15 —

Love Always Perseveres

Perseverance is not a long race; it is many short races one after another.

—Walter Elliott

Introduction

Love needs to be at its best when church is a mess, to paraphrase Paul's message to the church in Corinth. He began his list with patience and ended with its very close cousin—perseverance. In many ways, this takes us back to where we started—with the determination to live out a love that holds on, watches and waits, and leans in and grinds, always protecting, always trusting, always hoping, always persevering, even as God has extended that love to each of us. Indeed, love always perseveres.

Many of us think of perseverance as a very long, often exhausting race, but as the epigraph above suggests, perhaps it is better to think of it as a series of short races one after another in the same direction. In this chapter, we'll consider several of these short races, but first a story about a man who personified a holy perseverance in some messy situations.

Reuben Roberts[1]

Reuben Roberts lived in the hill country of Tennessee on a small farm about eight miles outside of Erin, the county seat of Houston County, just a mile or so down Tennessee Ridge and a short distance from the Tennessee River. The farm consisted of five eight-acre fields used mostly for growing soybeans and

---

1. First published in Allen, *For Today: A Prayer When Life Gets Messy* (Eugene, OR: Cascade, 2018).

hay, a small creek, a springhouse, two old weather-worn storage buildings, an outhouse, and 160 acres of old-growth hardwoods up on the hill, mostly walnut, oak, hickory, and ash. He and his large family lived in an old walnut log house built sometime just before the Civil War. They tell about the time that some of Grant's troops occupied the house for a time after the Battle of Fort Donelson over in Dover in 1862. They sat around the fireplace chewing and spitting tobacco, and the juice dripped through the floorboards, landing on Confederate soldiers hiding below. I don't know if that really happened, but it is certainly a good story, nonetheless. I bought that old farmhouse in the 1980s from one of Reuben's sons. On quiet winter evenings, I would sit by that same fireplace and imagine the conversations that went on so many years before. If only those old walls could talk . . .

In the Tennessee hills, funerals are something special to behold, and they are a celebration of community when an elder is laid to rest. There isn't much liturgy or pomp and circumstance, mostly stories, a few hymns, and shared remembrances—some good, some funny, mostly true. This was true of Reuben's funeral, too. During the service, a middle-aged man rose to speak. "Reuben Roberts was a good man," he began. "He was not only a good farmer, but a good preacher, too. As a young man, he was a circuit rider, a preacher with a horse and a Bible, filling the pulpit on alternate Sundays in Erin and Dixon. Once while returning from Dixon, he was stopped by an angry posse. It seems that someone had robbed, beaten, and otherwise mistreated a young woman in Dixon, and Reuben fit the general description of the perpetrator. The foreman of the posse led Reuben over to a nearby tree and put a rope around his neck. 'Before we hang you, do you have anything to say?' he asked. 'If so, now is the time to utter your last words.' So, Reuben did. He bowed his head and prayed. He prayed for his family, he prayed for his churches, he prayed for his neighbors, he prayed for himself, and then he prayed for his accusers. When he was through, he raised his head, looked the foreman in the eyes, and told him that he was as ready as he ever would be. The foreman cleared his throat, then turned to the posse and said, 'You'd better cut him down, boys, we've got the wrong man.' So, they did."

The storyteller continued, "I've heard that old story about a hundred times now, and told it more than a few times myself. You see, that foreman was my grandfather, and he never forgot the day he almost hung an innocent man. He always cautioned me to avoid judging a book by its cover. There is no doubt, Reuben Roberts was a good man."

As the middle-aged man sat down, a woman just a bit older stood to her feet. "Yes," she began in a matter-of-fact way, "Reuben Roberts was a good man. And not only was he a good preacher, he was a good neighbor, too. You see, late one bitterly cold winter's night, Reuben could not sleep. He woke up worried about his neighbors down the valley—about three miles away. As much as he tried, he couldn't rest, so he got up, dressed, saddled the horse, and headed off down the dirt road toward the river. Like Abraham, he obeyed and went, although he didn't know exactly where he was going or why. As he approached his neighbor's cabin, he saw a dim, flickering light in the window. When he knocked on the door, a small girl appeared and simply began to cry. You see, her daddy was gone and her mother was desperately ill with the flu, near death. There was no food in the house, and the firewood was almost gone. Reuben brought in some wood and stoked the fire. He told the girl that he would return shortly. He rode back to his farm, got his wife out of bed, and sent her back to the neighbor's cabin with some hot food and comfort. He then set off for the town eight miles in the other direction to fetch the doctor. Of course, the doctor was not excited about heading out into the hills on such a terribly cold night, but Reuben persisted. He mentioned later that he had to part with a butchered hog to get his neighbor some help, but he was glad to do so."

The women looked around at those sitting in the church and said in earnest, "I know this happened because I was the little girl in the cabin that night. Truly, Reuben Roberts was a good man."

Slowly, an even older man stood to speak. Stabilizing himself by leaning on his cane and the back of the pew in front of him, he started in a slow but steady voice, "Reuben Roberts was not only a good man and a good neighbor, he was a generous one, too. You see, Reuben also worked for the county as the road commissioner during the depression. In those days that mostly meant supervising the road crew as they graded the roads with a blade pulled by a team of mules. One day as they were grading a back road, Reuben saw a young farmer plowing an adjacent field with a two-horse team. Reuben told the road crew to stop and rest as he climbed over the fence to talk to the farmer. 'I don't know exactly why I am doing this,' he told the young farmer, 'but I feel like I should give you this.' He pulled out a five-dollar bill from his pocket and handed it to the farmer.

In those days, five dollars was real money. Tears streamed down the farmer's face as he stared at the money in his hand. 'Thank you so much, sir. I don't know how you knew, but last winter was such a terrible one for us. It was so bad, in fact, that we had to eat our seed corn to survive, and this is enough money to buy the seed we need for planting season. I don't know how I can ever repay you.'" The old man finished by saying, "Yes, I know it sounds beyond belief, but I know it happened because I was the young farmer who received that remarkable gift. Reuben Roberts was a good man, indeed. May he rest in peace."

It was as if the benediction had been pronounced. The locals began to disperse from the church, and I quickly made my way across the parking lot and over to the old farmer who told the story about having no seed corn before he could climb into his pickup and drive off. "That was a miracle!" I blurted out. "Yes," he agreed, "how he knew I was in need of seed for planting and generous enough to part with his money during that terrible depression is a true miracle."

"Oh," I said, "the fact that Reuben was sensitive to God's prompting and generous enough to follow through is certainly a wonderful story, but that's not the miracle that I am talking about. No, the miracle for me is that you were out there plowing your fields when you didn't have any seed to plant, plowing without any guarantee of a crop to harvest in the fall. Now, that's a miracle!"

The old farmer just looked up at me with misty eyes, nodded, and smiled at me as I asked, "What made you go out to the barn and hitch up a team in such circumstances? Why would anyone do that without having any seeds to plant?"

"Well," the old farmer said as he gazed off into the distance, "there are times in life when all you can do is get out of bed and step into the work that calls you—and not think about much else. You go to work where you are with what you've got, and you do what you can. If nothing else, perseverance has its own reward."

Yes, indeed.

* * *

Perseverance in Three Short Races

The story of Reuben Roberts highlights three of the short races that love calls us to run, especially when church is a mess. The first has to do with misunderstandings, gossip, and downright meanness. What do we do when others misconstrue our motives, talk behind our backs, misjudge our character, or work to undermine our standing and our reputations, even in an attempt to run us off or take our jobs? Honestly, what can we do? Of course, our first instinct is to fight back, to respond in kind, an eye for an eye, but that seldom does anything other than to make matters worse. At the end of the day, it is up to others who know us to ferret out the truth and to defend us. Perhaps like Reuben Roberts, the best thing we can do is to simply live in such a way that no one will believe the nasty things said about us, and to pray for those who are doing the talking. This may seem naive, but I believe that it is the most powerful response there is. Sometimes, love calls us to persevere by simply going about our business with our heads held high and our integrity intact—and by praying for those who persecute us, as Jesus instructed his followers to do (Matt 5:44).

At other times, love call us to persevere by making sacrifices for those in need. When Reuben Roberts promised the doctor a butchered hog for assisting a neighbor in need, that was no small sacrifice, especially in the depth of the Great Depression. Giving up a mature hog cost him and his family dearly, something real, and he even had to pay for the butchering and delivery! In the midst of a messy church situation, needs arise but few are willing to step up and help. Why? Because there is a real cost for doing so and many are occupied with "more important and pressing" issues. Still, one or two couples (usually the same one or two couples) will lean in and help out, and there is always a cost for doing so. There are rewards, too, eternal rewards, because perseverance in the form of sacrificial giving is love at its best when it is needed the most.

And sometimes, love calls us to persevere by simply hitching up the mule team and heading to the fields, even when we have nothing to plant. I think we've all been there at one time or another—no gas in the tank, no wind in our sails, no idea of where our work will take us or why we are doing what we are doing in the first place. It is in these times that God honors small steps, weary but faithful steps, just one foot in front of the other. Of course, there are no guarantees that someone will jump the fence and give us five dollars for seed, thus solving all our immediate problems, but I believe that God honors our perseverance in ways known and unknown. We take small steps, believing that God will do the heavy lifting. In the end, our perseverance takes us somewhere, even if like Abraham, we do not know where we are going (Heb 11:8).

Scripture

As we look to Scripture for some insights about perseverance, I want to focus on an aspect of perseverance that is rarely discussed, even a bit counterintuitive—knowing when it is time to pass the torch and step away or move on. Granted, it is possible to step away from a difficult task or a church too soon, but perseverance doesn't demand that we stay in one place forever. That's ego and stubbornness speaking. Most of us can think of a pastor or a boss who stayed in an assignment far too long, and everyone breathed a sigh of relief when they finally retired. It seems that retirements can be celebrated for a variety of reasons. And the problem is not new. The Old Testament gives us many examples of passing the torch, but we'll focus on Moses.

Moses and Joshua

Of course, Moses was a strong and exceptional leader, one of the most familiar personalities in all of the Old Testament. When you have a movie made about your travails and Charlton Heston plays your part, you know you've done some big things. Moses experienced almost every kind of high and low you can think of, and yet he was faithful to lead the children of Israel to the promised land—or at least in view of it. He had every intention of leading the effort to cross the Jordan River and claim the land, but God told him that his time of leadership was over. His assistant, Joshua, would take over and finish the journey. It must have been terribly disappointing to Moses after all those years in the desert, but instead of pouting or arguing, giving all the reasons he could think of as to why he should finish the task rather than Joshua, he called everyone together and said: "I am now a hundred and twenty years old and I am no longer able to lead you. The Lord has said to me, 'You shall not cross the Jordan'" (Deut 31:2).

A simple, straightforward message, and as he passed the torch to Joshua, he blessed and affirmed his leadership in their presence: "Then Moses summoned Joshua and said to him in the presence of all Israel, 'Be strong and courageous, for you must go with this people into the land that the Lord swore to their ancestors to give them, and you must divide it among them as their inheritance. The Lord himself goes before you and will be with you; he will never leave you nor forsake you. Do not be afraid; do not be discouraged'" (Deut 31:7–8).

This is a powerful act of leadership, but extremely difficult for many leaders to do. It takes humility and wisdom to step down gracefully and affirm, empower, and bless your successor, especially when you did not want to step down in the first place. Truly, it is a wise leader (or follower) who prays for wisdom to know when to step away, and to do so gracefully when the time comes. It is a prayer for us all since that time comes for all of us.

As it turns out, the last obligation of a leader is to make a graceful exit, even when the situation is a mess. Often, we can get so caught up in the mess that it takes someone else with a fresh perspective to see a way forward. Paul is clear that love always perseveres, and sometimes the next short race of perseverance is to gracefully pass the torch and move on.

Next Steps

Let me offer four next steps as we consider that love always perseveres, especially when church is a mess. First, *recalibrate*. Rather than thinking of perseverance as doggedly persisting in an endeavor, as a never-ending and exhausting race with no exit plan, think of persevering as a series of short races one after another in the same direction or with the same intent. When we do, it diminishes the idea that perseverance is a single lifetime activity, leaving us with no options or choices to make along the way. We do have options and we can make choices.

Second, *focus* on the next short story, not on the future or the entire story of your life. Stay tuned to what is happening now, not on failings or failures in years past or on some type of legacy due to long service. I have known many who knew that a major change was in order but wanted to complete a certain number of years of service, say twenty or thirty or even fifty. Really, would eighteen or twenty-eight or forty-seven years have been any different, other than for their own sense of perseverance? I don't think so, and when the focus becomes the number of years we have served rather than the task before us, it's probably time to pass the torch.

Third, *be sensitive and prayerful* about the proper time to pass the torch and enlist a close friend or advisor who will be honest and courageous enough to tell you when the shelf life on your current work has expired. It's not comfortable to send or receive such messages, but it is good to have the process in place before it is needed. And if you serve in a messy situation, it is fitting to have a formal process in place where the issue of the length of your stay can be safely and fairly discussed. Over the years, five or six individuals have asked me to tell them when it was time to pass the torch and move on. I did so twice, and in both instances, they became very angry and defensive. So, if you ask for someone to tell you the truth, you have to be willing to accept the message without shooting the messenger. Better to pass the torch two years early than one year too late.

Finally, *pass the torch with grace.* Just do it and do you best to affirm and encourage your successor as you go. This is the last obligation of a leader or volunteer, and it may be one of the hardest things we will ever be asked to do. But love always perseveres—for those we are leaving and in our next short story, too.

Conclusion

The Apostle Paul started his list of qualities for a love at its best with patience (love is patient) and ended with perseverance (love always perseveres). They are related, but they are not the same thing. Patience is the virtue that encourages perseverance through difficult and messy situations—malicious talk, sacrificial giving, and running out of gas along the way, to name just three. It is important, however, to think of perseverance as a series of short life stories one after the other rather than an endless trek with no exit. Honestly, life doesn't work that way.

Passing the torch and moving on is also an aspect of perseverance, a part of life. Moses had to pass the torch to Joshua on the very eve of the crossing into the promised land. It wasn't by choice, but he did so with grace and dignity. He affirmed Joshua's leadership and encouraged his people. There's a lesson there for all of us.

At the end of the day, there will be an end of the day for whatever we undertake, so we can either pass the torch or have it taken from us or watch it slowly diminish and go out. We get to run our own race, but not necessarily under circumstances of our own choosing. Love always perseveres, Paul tells us, and we will, too, even as we start our next short race. And we have the assurance that we will never be alone. Love simply won't allow it.

Questions for Reflection and Discussion:

1. What do you see as the difference between patience and perseverance? How are they related?
2. Is it helpful to think of perseverance as a series of short races rather than one life-long race? Why or why not?
3. Have you ever faced a spiritual task but realized that you were simply out of gas, with no wind in your sails, having no seed corn to plant? How did you manage this tough time? What got you through? What did you learn from the experience?
4. Can you think of a time when a leader stayed too long and became part of the problem rather than part of the way forward? How did it finally resolve itself?
5. Is there a torch that you need to pass? What is preventing you from doing so? What might be your next steps?

Love is patient, love is kind. It does not envy, it does not boast,
it is not proud. It does not dishonor others, it is not self-seeking,
it is not easily angered, it keeps no record of wrongs.
Love does not delight in evil but rejoices with the truth.
It always protects, always trusts, always hopes, always perseveres. . . .

—— CONCLUSION ——

Love Never Fails

Love recognizes no barriers. It jumps hurdles, leaps fences, penetrates walls to arrive at its destination full of hope.

—Maya Angelou

When church is a mess, we need something we can count on, something to carry and comfort us, and honestly there aren't many. Much like the church in Corinth, we tend to rely on our own spiritual gifts, talents, and knowledge to prop up our spirits and our egos to get us through, but the Apostle Paul is clear: "where there are prophecies, they will cease; where there are tongues, they will be stilled; where there is knowledge, it will pass away" (1 Cor 13:8). As it turns out, none of us are as wise as we think we are or would like to be. Paul tells us that we only see and know in part (13:12). In other words, we don't know it all and never will—none of us, not even Paul.

So, clearly we can't count on our own spirituality when we find ourselves or our church in a mess, but we can count on love. Love never fails. And when love is at its best, it is grounded in patience and kindness, virtues that can be learned and practiced. And this love is not rude, angry, proud, boastful, or petty, but always protects, trusts, hopes, and perseveres. These qualities are challenging, but they can be intentionally practiced, too, even in a mess, and we get better at them as we do.

Writing to another congregation, Paul summarized his thoughts on love this way: "And over all these virtues put on love, which binds them all together in perfect unity. Let the peace of Christ rule in your hearts, since as members of one body you were called to peace. And be thankful" (Col 3:14–15). This is good advice for all of us as we face our messes, even if they are of our own doing. Love at its best binds us together and brings unity, so put it on. In other words, wear it, use it, practice it. It is the glue that holds all things together. And when we do, peace is possible; we can't manufacture it, but it will come. And as we look back at the messes we have faced or are facing right now, we can be thankful—thankful for the goodness and grace that goes before us, is with us in the mess, and in us, too. Gratitude can always be summoned regardless of where we are or what we face, because above all, love never fails—never. Thanks be to God.

Paul concluded his thoughts on love at its best this way: "And now these three remain: faith, hope and love. But the greatest of these is love (1 Cor 13:13). No argument here. I like to think of it this way: Faith sends us on a spiritual journey; hope keeps us going; and love bids us home.

Journey well.

Love is patient, love is kind. It does not envy, it does not boast,
it is not proud. It does not dishonor others, it is not self-seeking,
it is not easily angered, it keeps no record of wrongs.
Love does not delight in evil but rejoices with the truth.
It always protects, always trusts, always hopes, always perseveres.
Love never fails.

www.ingramcontent.com/pod-product-compliance
Lightning Source LLC
Chambersburg PA
CBHW030113170426
43198CB00009B/603